HAPPY IS THE MAN . . .

HAPPY
is the
MAN ....

 Robert V. Ozment

FLEMING H. REVELL COMPANY

FOR MY WIFE *Arah,* AND
MY TWO SONS *Randall* AND *Richard,*
WHO HAVE BROUGHT HAPPINESS, JOY
AND GLADNESS TO MY LIFE

CONTENTS

HAPPY IS THE MAN . . .

1

The Wrong Roads to Happiness

EVERYBODY WANTS to be happy. I have never met anyone who was willing to live in a state of frustration and misery. It is only natural that man's desire for happiness provides both the strength and the purpose to explore paths that he feels will lead to the land of happiness.

Webster's dictionary defines happiness as: "A state of well-being and pleasurable satisfaction. . . ." To accept such a broad definition, for our purpose, would lead to confusion. Happiness, in this sense, could only be short-lived; even the seed from which it grew might be tainted with evil and sown in the shallow soil of selfishness. It might burst forth and bloom for a short time and then die from the lack of refreshing rains of service and the rich spiritual soil of purpose.

For example, a criminal may feel a sudden surge of happiness when one of his underworld enemies falls under the cruel blow of death. A bank robber may feel the fresh breezes of simulative happiness after successfully carrying out his plan to take something to which he had no right. But can these feelings truly be termed "happiness"?

When I was doing research on the Bowery in New York City, I could not help noticing how the face of an alcoholic would light up with happiness when someone gave him the price of a drink. He would hurry away to the nearest bar in an effort to escape from himself and the problems of his world. It is easy to see that we must search for a higher form of happiness than a dictionary describes, or the search will lead to utter defeat and indescribable misery.

Bertrand Russell, in one of his books, wrote a chapter entitled

"Is Happiness Still Possible?" My first reaction to such a title was, "How absurd can one be?" Happiness is always possible, yet many people never find the road that leads to it. Recently, it was reported that there were over 36,000 suicides in the United States in one year. The unfortunate victims could not find their way through the jungle of frustration and confusion to peace and happiness. Though our first reaction to such a statistic is that the suicides probably occurred among downtrodden and impoverished people, the fact is that a multitude of the victims lived in lovely mansions and controlled great wealth. True, some were mentally deranged; others faced problems that were too big for them, and they did not know where to turn to find help; still others had a confused sense of values.

There are plenty of facts that would make an interesting debate on Russell's chapter, "Is Happiness Still Possible?" The young person in this country who is now twenty years old has lived all of his life either in a world of war or under the constant threat of global disaster. His lifetime has witnessed some marvelous events, but it has also been a period of ceaseless stress and unparalleled strain. Can young people of this era find happiness? Yes, there is only one answer to the question, "Is Happiness Possible?" Jesus gave it to us: "I have overcome the world" (JOHN 16:33). What did Jesus mean? Did He not mean that He had learned to live a serene, happy, confident life in spite of the world? Did He not mean that He had learned to live in the world, yet live above all that is evil?

More than fifty per cent of all patients who crowd the nation's hospitals are suffering from mental disorders. Our nation is blessed with over seven thousand hospitals, but most of the time one's name must be placed on a waiting list to gain entrance unless the nature of his illness is classified as an emergency.

The greater number of the large cities in our nation have found it necessary to build more prisons in order to care for criminals. I am aware of the fact that there is a great influx of

12

people moving into the cities, but the rate of urban crime is increasing in a larger proportion than the growth of urban population. The people who fill our jails have a distorted sense of values. The newspapers reported recently that a young man, who left a trail of crime from one coast to the other, stated when asked why he did it, "I was just trying to put a little fun in my life."

There are two levels of happiness, and the human heart is capable of living on either one. One level is what I choose to call mundane happiness; the other is divine happiness.

Let's take a look at mundane happiness: it is short-lived, temporary, mostly superficial, and has the ring of emptiness about it. A man's face may register happiness when his employer calls him in and tells him about a substantial promotion which carries with it a corresponding increase in salary. A woman may be thrilled with joy when she unwraps what she guesses is a pair of pajamas and housecoat, only to find a mink stole. Did you ever look at a little child's face on Christmas morning? His eyes, his smile and his actions express the gladness his heart knows. A young girl gains the attention of the young man in her life and she becomes ecstatically happy.

There is nothing wrong with this level of happiness as long as we see it for what it is worth. It is merely a form of delight which is easily lost among the memories of yesterday. There is hardly a sight more beautiful than a field of morning-glories, with the sparkle of dew shining on each blossom. Yet, a florist never uses this flower in a corsage or bouquet. Surely, it is not because the morning-glory lacks color and beauty. The reason is simply that the blossoms will not last. By the time the sun evaporates the dew drops, and the freshness of the morning is gone, this delicate flower loses its luster.

Worldly happiness depends upon our circumstances; we are at the mercy of our likes and dislikes. The waters of adversity make us sad; personal achievements and possessions make us glad. God knows that it is impossible for us to live constantly

13

in the land of mundane happiness. There are times when we must walk in the valley of loneliness and up the slopes of sadness.

Now let us examine divine happiness. It is difficult to achieve this level, and it comes only to those who are willing to pay the price of complete dedication. God is the inexhaustible Source of divine happiness. When we follow the Master faithfully through the dark Garden of Gethsemane, the unjust halls of Pilate, and struggle with Him up the rugged slopes of Calvary, we feel the indescribable and ceaseless surge of divine happiness in our lives.

The happiness which God puts in the human heart is tough and strong. When He lights the torch of divine happiness in human lives, it will shine in every dark night and guide us safely through the storms of life. The winds of sickness may blow, but that divine light will remind us that God is near. We will hear afresh the words that Jesus spoke to His frustrated disciples: "Peace I leave with you, my peace I give unto you: not as the world giveth, give I unto you. Let not your heart be troubled, neither let it be afraid" (JOHN 14:27).

The black clouds of sorrow will inevitably flood our lives some day and the load of grief will press heavily upon our souls. At first, we will feel deserted, but that divine light will give us assurance as we experience the presence of God. Then, we will know the truth of our Lord's words: "I will not leave you comfortless: I will come to you" (JOHN 14:18).

The rains of temptation will come; there is no fallout shelter to protect us from them. We need not yield to the desires of the heart and seek to satisfy the drives of the flesh. If we are sensitive to the voice of God, all the rains of temptation can never extinguish His divine light. With the psalmist we can say, "Thou shalt guide me with thy counsel, and afterward receive me to glory" (PSALMS 73:24).

On my desk I have a letter from a lady in a nursing home. She writes, "I am an old woman. I shall be ninety years old the seventeenth of June. I am in the sunset of life and soon my stay on earth will be over. Don't think I'm here with a long face and complaining, because I'm not. I am happy, and I know that as soon as my stay is over here, I will go Home and live forever." This letter expresses the genuine Christian happiness that can be found only when we walk with God. This lady knows the kind of happiness that will not diminish with time; it has kept her steady during the storms of life. God helps us to achieve this level of happiness.

Mundane happiness grows thin and quickly loses its glow. Genuine happiness, which has its source in God, will never lose its luster. The difference is like that between a polluted pond and a rippling stream: when water is still, it becomes lifeless and a breeding place for mosquitoes; a babbling brook is fresh, because the water is continually moving, and it cannot become stagnant.

Some years back, Catherine Mackenzie reported the result of a scholastic-opinion poll in which high-school students were invited to consider some long-range goals. Only four per cent wanted to make a lot of money. The overwhelming majority stated that they wanted "to live a simple but secure and happy life without making a lot of money or becoming famous." It is encouraging that many of our youth can lift their sights above the mounting tide of materialism and see some worthy goals.

Epictetus, the Greek philosopher, said, "God made all men to be happy." The results of happiness substantiate this belief. A happy worker produces more and better work than one who feels miserable. But happiness is achieved after we observe certain laws. Remember, happiness is not a gift; it is an achievement.

Once a young lady gave a piano recital. She proved to be an accomplished musician, and after the recital one of the guests asked, "Mary, how did you learn to play so beautifully?" The young lady was quite frank in her reply: "It took me many months of hard work. I practiced, and practiced, and practiced." She was willing to pay the price of perseverance in order to become a good musician.

15

Divine happiness is man's greatest challenge; at the same time it represents man's greatest achievement. We have learned to produce atomic and hydrogen bombs. Our scientists have learned to orbit men around the earth; outer space is no longer a fathomless mystery. The achievements of the past are astonishing, but the lessons we have failed to learn could defeat us.

Charles Steinmetz was correct when he said, "Some day people will learn that material things do not bring happiness and are of little use in making men and women creative and powerful. Then the scientists of the world will turn their laboratories over to the study of God and prayer and the spiritual forces which, as yet, have been hardly scratched. When that day comes, the world will see more advancement in one generation than it has seen in the last four."

The trouble with most people who are looking for happiness is that they search in the wrong places. Let us consider some roads that people travel in their quests for happiness and that will certainly lead to deception and disappointment.

Some individuals think that happiness comes out of reaching desired goals. It is true that one feels a deep sense of accomplishment when he has attained a certain goal in life, but this sort of happiness is always temporary.

I know a young man who thought his world would look rosy if he could only leave high school. He achieved his goal and was exceedingly happy for a short time. Later, when confronted with greater problems than daily study, he found himself depressed and unhappy again.

Almost every month I talk with young people who want to get married. Some of them are still in high school; I always discourage high-school students from marrying. Most of them feel that marriage will bring unsurpassed happiness, but, according to the records of our divorce courts, a teen-aged marriage frequently brings misery and heartache. On my desk is a letter from a young girl in Arkansas, who writes, "I was so stubborn that I failed to see the wisdom of my parents. I married at sixteen, thinking I would find married bliss. I have been miserably unhappy ever since. If I had my life to live over, I would certainly listen to the advice of my parents." Then she told me some of her domestic troubles and closed her letter by asking, "Can you give me some advice that might make our marriage work?" I advised her to go to her pastor or a marriage counseling service. I also offered these suggestions: (1) Attend church regularly; (2) ask God at the beginning of each day to guide you; (3) talk to your husband in a spirit of love, in an effort to heal old wounds; (4) close the day on your knees, asking God to forgive your mistakes and help you to live a better life tomorrow.

Genuine happiness that will last longer than a few weeks will not come simply because we have attained some of our goals. Worthy goals ought to be steppingstones to a better life as well as a higher happiness.

Some people seem to think that happiness grows out of their possessions. Ours is the richest country in the world, as far as material things are concerned. A recent survey disclosed that ninety-eight per cent of the homes in America have one or more radios, and the number of television sets and other expensive appliances is equally impressive. But can we truthfully say that money has made us happy?

A few months ago a realtor asked me if I knew of a prospective buyer for a luxurious home. He explained the property in these terms: "There are two acres of beautiful rolling lawn. The grounds have been landscaped to perfection. The house is of fine architectural design. It has four bedrooms and four baths. It was constructed of the finest old brick available, and much of the interior material was hand-selected. The home has a three-car garage and servants' quarters. In the back it has a fine swimming pool, a large patio and a fireplace. It's really a mansion if I have ever seen one." When I asked, "Why are the people selling," the realtor replied, "They are getting a divorce."

If happiness is the result of "things," and many people seem to think this is true, then the family who owned that home

17

should have been ecstatically happy. All too frequently misery lives in a mansion and is fed from a golden spoon. I do not mean that you cannot be both rich and happy. What I do mean is that if you are both rich and happy, you are not happy simply because you are rich.

In contrast to luxurious living, I remember many rural homes I visited when I served as a student pastor. The people whom I served were poor, if you measure wealth by a financial yardstick. Most of them had no bank accounts; they lived off the food they raised. When I called on one family, I could feel the love and happiness they knew. The living room was furnished with a table, an oil-burning lamp and four cane-bottomed chairs. "Come on in, preacher," said my host, "we are poor but happy, and you are welcome."

I asked a friend, a noted psychiatrist, to give me a breakdown on his patients as to their economic standing. "About eighty per cent of my patients are upper class, fifteen per cent are upper-middle class, and about five per cent are middle class," he replied. This does not prove that poor and lower-middle-class people do not feel the load of misery and unhappiness; it may simply prove that they cannot afford a psychiatrist. But it does give evidence to the fact that money will not make us immune from unhappiness. The truth is, I know a great many people who live in poverty—and as many who have wealth—who are genuinely happy. You are never happy because of what you have, but because of what you are.

A few years ago, I was called to counsel with a very wealthy man who was near death. He had lived a long time and his only interests were counting his money and watching the stock market. He had managed to build a sizable financial fortune during his lifetime, but he had woefully neglected his spiritual life. He knew that death would take him out of his little world of selfishness and, now, at the twilight, he turned his mind to things of an eternal nature. He was no longer interested in the stocks and bonds he owned; they could not comfort him. He lifted his eyes beyond the glitter of earthly possessions in search of eternal values. "The hour is late," he said, "and I want to know about God."

I told the dying man about the love of God as expressed on Calvary, and about God's forgiveness. His eyes lighted up and he asked, "Will God accept me?" How could I answer a question like that? Here was a man who had neglected God for several decades. He had been a wayward child most of his life. There is only one answer, and I did not hesitate to give it to him: "God will take you." That is the gospel. There is a danger about waiting, because we might not be as lucky as that man. He had time to regret that he missed living in this world, but he left with the assurance that he would live throughout eternity.

I told the repentant man about the thief who died on the cross next to that of our Lord. The sick man, whose face had been covered with fear and confusion, smiled. I saw on his face the joy that Christ had brought to his heart.

We must look beyond the glitter of the world if we want to achieve divine happiness. God wants us to be happy, but most of us are traveling the wrong road. We must serve others as well as work for ourselves; we must give to others as well as receive from them; we must search for happiness in what we are, rather than in what we have. There is no genuine happiness without God.

2

Five Steps to Real Happiness

ONCE I WAS speaking to a convention of businessmen in Florida and, after I had finished, one of my listeners invited me to have some coffee with him in the hotel dining room. I could tell by the look on his face that he wanted to talk about something important, so I accepted his invitation. By the time we were comfortably seated, he said, "I wish I could be as happy as I believe you are."

"You can be," I assured him. "Tell me about yourself."

Here are some of the things I learned about him. He was a well-educated and modest man. His health was good, and he had been extremely successful. He had a lovely wife and three small children. He owned his own home and was being promoted at an accelerated pace in his company. He and his wife were deeply in love. You might think that such good fortune would assure a man of genuine happiness.

My final question to this man concerned his relationship to God. "I was afraid you would ask me about that," he replied. "I haven't been to church since high school, and have become skeptical about God and religion," he continued. "You had better be thankful," I told him, "that God has not become skeptical about you. He still believes in you, and you will never find spiritual peace until you bring God back into your life."

If happiness means the absence of sorrow, pain, disappointment and trouble, then you and I cannot possibly be happy from the moment we enter life until we set sail for the shores of eternity. If happiness is simply a continuous state of excitement, thrills, pleasure and satisfaction, it remains an impossible goal to attain. Sorrow, pain and discomfort seem to be as much a part

21

of life as gladness, good health and contentment. Some have tried to live on mountain peaks of excitement, pleasure and thrills, but this form of happiness eventually brings weariness and it ultimately is broken by the inevitable tragedies of life.

If, on the other hand, happiness reflects the unceasing love of God, His forgiveness, His God-given strength to bear the loads of grief and pain in life, and the confident knowledge that we are now and forever in His hands, then happiness is possible. It is within the reach of every living soul. The cost of this kind of happiness, which I choose to call genuine Christian happiness, is the same for all.

Some people seem to feel that good health and pleasant circumstances will produce divine happiness. Fanny J. Crosby became blind when she was very young. Now blindness, as far as I am concerned, is one of life's greatest physical handicaps, yet Fanny Crosby has been, through her many wonderful hymns, a successful servant of God. She has pointed the way to God for an uncounted number of confused and lost people. She once wrote, "I am the happiest soul living. If I had not been deprived of my sight, I would never have received so good an education, nor cultivated so fine a memory, nor have been able to do good to so many people."

With a firm faith in God we can always reap the fruit of divine happiness regardless of our health or surrounding circumstances. When General William Booth was told that he was losing his sight and would soon be totally blind, he said to his son, "I have done what I could for God and the people with two eyes. Now I will do what I can for God and the people without eyes."

When Henry Fawcett was a young man he lost both eyes in a shooting accident. This young Englishman determined that such a handicap would not cause him to give up the important business of living. "I made up my mind," he wrote, "within ten minutes after the accident, to stick to my main purpose so far as in me lay."

22

Robert Louis Stevenson went through life with a weak body. He spent most of his life suffering, but he did not retreat into a life of self-pity and uselessness. His life has been an inspiration to many, and his writings will offer hope to men as long as great literature is read.

The late Dr. William P. King related the story of a very wealthy woman who was unhappy and restless in spite of her financial fortune. She told her maid that she felt that a change of scenery was all she needed. She even suggested a place where, because of its beauty and pleasant surroundings, she could lose her despair and find happiness. The maid, who had no formal education, expressed a very wise and true philosophy: "No, ma'am, you surely would not be happy there, because you'd have to take yourself with you wherever you went."

A casual look at history will reveal a gallant army of physically handicapped men and women who have marched across the stage of life, bearing triumph on their faces and gladness in their hearts. If they could rise above their handicaps, we can rise above ours. We cannot do it alone. We must have God.

After the long hard day during which Jesus fed the multitude, He sent His disciples across the Sea of Galilee to Bethsaida. Jesus went into the mountains to be alone with His Father in prayer. Later, He went to join His disciples. The Sea of Galilee can be very dangerous, and on this particular night the wind was strong and the waves high. The disciples were struggling to keep the little ship on its course.

When the men saw Jesus approaching them, walking on the water, they were filled with fear. What they said is not recorded, but I imagine they called out in prayer for divine help. Immediately Jesus spoke to them: "Be of good cheer: it is I; be not afraid" (MARK 6:50). Another translation of the words of Jesus might read: "Be happy, be glad—do not be afraid. I am here."

Christians today encounter contrary winds and face deep disappointments. We sometimes feel the heavy and almost crushing blow of sorrow upon our shoulders. We do indeed

23

know what it is to struggle against fierce temptations in life. It is an endless task to keep the ships of our souls on a true course.

I want to suggest five steps that will lead to divine happiness. These are not easy steps to take, and the tenderfoot might wish to remain behind.

(1) The first step is to be grateful for the gifts of the moment. I do not mean that you should sit in idle contentment with the present; I mean that you should be grateful for your situation, for it could become worse. If you cannot be grateful for the present gifts, you will not likely be grateful when your lot improves. Misery and unhappiness grow in the soil of ingratitude.

Once a little boy was playing with only one roller skate. It was quite obvious that he was having a grand time. A man watching the lad commented, "Sonny, you ought to have two skates." The little fellow grinned and replied, "Sure, mister. I know I ought to have two skates, but you can have an awful good time on one skate if that's all you've got."

Kenneth Hildebrand, in *Achieving Real Happiness*, related the story about a young girl who suddenly lost both her parents in death. She had lived all of her life in the country, but she was brought to the crowded city to live with a large family. The adjustments were difficult; she became despondent and shy. One day, as the girl was sitting on the front steps of the home, a kindly lady walked by and noticed the dejected look on her face. The woman patted the youngster on the head and said, "Life ain't all you want, but it's all you got. So, stick a daisy in your hat and be happy." These words from a kind old lady put fresh hope into the girl's life and she sought and found a job the next day. It was the beginning of a new life for a girl who had retreated into self-pity.

A letter came recently from an old man in the Midwest. He wrote about his suffering, and many long and sleepless nights. He has lost his legs, and any hope that he might walk again, even with artificial limbs, is dim. "Don't think I'm complaining," he wrote. "I thank God every day for His love and good-

24

ness. God has been my strength and my source of happiness through the long journey of life."

It would be hard to defeat a man with such a wonderful spirit of gratitude in his heart, even when he walks through the valley of pain and approaches the shadow of death. We become the slaves of unhappiness and misery when we take the attitude that life has cheated us or that we have been neglected by the divine Hand that created us.

If you want to achieve divine happiness, take this first step: thank God for the gifts of the present which He has so generously showered upon you. Above all, don't linger in the regrets of the past. The psalmist said, "Enter into his gates with thanksgiving, and into his courts with praise: be thankful unto him, and bless his name" (PSALMS 100:4).

(2) If divine happiness is to be ours, we must learn to master our thoughts. In a large measure we can determine our futures. The writer of Proverbs wrote, "For as he [man] thinketh in his heart, so is he" (23:7). We set the mood of each day by our attitudes and thoughts toward the things we must do.

I am well aware of the fact that we cannot simply think our troubles away. On the other hand, I do believe that we create many problems by negative thinking. We must face reality, but at the same time we do not need to manufacture problems with our skepticism.

Once a little girl, after a wonderful day of play, reminded her mother at bedtime, "I have had such a happy time today!"

"I am glad," her mother responded, "but tell me, what made this day any different from yesterday?" After a short pause, the little girl replied, "Well, yesterday I let my thoughts push me around, and today I pushed my thoughts around."

That is the story of many adult lives. We permit our unchristian thoughts to push us around and direct our lives. A lady once responded to my question, "How has the day gone for you?" by saying, "It has been simply horrible, and I expect tomorrow will be the same. My life," she continued, "has been one series of

25

disappointments after another. Nothing seems to go right." This baffled me, because I barely knew the lady, but I decided to try something.

"I know that positive thinking will not cause your problems to disappear," I advised, "but it will change your attitude toward life in general, and toward your problems specifically. Tomorrow morning when you get up, say a little prayer. Ask God to make this a good day and to show you how you can help to make it one. Then, believe that things will go right for you." With a bit of sarcasm in her voice, she said, "I've tried everything else. I might as well try your suggestion."

A few weeks later the woman called me on the telephone. "I want to thank you," she began. "I have tried your suggestion and it works. I have a different outlook on life. You were absolutely right—positive thinking and prayer have not greatly changed my problems, but they have given me a new lease on life. At least, I am not creating more problems by looking on the dark side of every situation." She is learning the art of conquering her problems by living above them.

(3) If divine happiness is to be ours, we must do something for others. God did not make us to live in a world of selfishness; we must reach out and help others. The great French philosopher Blaise Pascal wrote, "The man who lives only for himself hates nothing so much as being alone with himself."

Jesus was never idle. He was busy continually helping others. Once He said, "For even the Son of man came not to be ministered unto, but to minister, and to give his life a ransom for many" (MARK 10:45). Again, Jesus said, ". . . I am among you as he that serveth" (LUKE 22:27).

Many wonderful things have been said about our Lord. He has been called Teacher, Redeemer, Master and Lord. I have an idea that Jesus feels greatly complimented when we call Him the Servant. He said, "For I came down from heaven, not to do mine own will, but the will of him that sent me" (JOHN 6:38). He is indeed humanity's greatest Servant.

26

Christianity is a place of refuge, but it is also a supply depot. It must not become simply a resting place. Unless it can be seen by the way we live that we know Christ, it will be exceedingly difficult, if not impossible, by mere words to convince others that we are Christians.

We must never become so engaged with our own petty problems and selfish interests that we forget the multitudes who are lost and without God. Divine happiness is possible only when we offer ourselves to help bind up the wounds of others.

(4) The next step in achieving divine happiness is placing our trust in God. The writer of Proverbs gives us a clue to this thought: ". . . whoso trusteth in the Lord, happy is he" (16:20). The psalmist warned us not to put our trust in princes. "Happy is he," wrote the psalmist, "that hath the God of Jacob for his help, whose hope is in the Lord his God" (146:5).

Everyone has in his possession a generous supply of faith. I have often heard people say, "I guess I just don't have enough faith." This is not an accurate statement. What they ought to say is this: "I guess I am just afraid to use my faith." Dr. Charles L. Allen, in *Healing Words*, says, "Faith is like a boomerang; begin using what you have and it comes back to you in greater measure."

All progress rests upon faith. Even scientific achievements have come about because of faith. For example, before we put a man in orbit around the earth, someone thought of the idea. He must have said to himself, "I believe man can orbit the earth." Now, the truth is, that man was not sure it could be done, but he began to work on the project because of his faith.

"Faith is betting your life that there is a God," wrote Donald Hankey. Faith is more: it is betting your life that God is fair and that God loves each one of us. Jesus was not afraid of the cross. He did not relish the suffering and agony it would bring, but He walked to the cross with a serene mind because He trusted in the wisdom of His Father.

God can be trusted. Everything I see points to this truth: the

27

universe is orderly and dependable; there is an intelligent Mind behind us. God does not waste anything: man is more than mud and water, flesh and blood; he has a mind and a soul. Across the centuries and down the corridors of time, God has been the same. He stands ready to bless, forgive, provide strength for, and redeem humanity. The writer of Hebrews wrote, "Jesus Christ the same yesterday, and to day, and for ever" (13:8).

Jesus, whose compassion led Him to heal the sick, restore sight to the blind, and forgive the woman caught in adultery, is here to bind up our wounds and send us away with a new song in our hearts. On his seventieth birthday, William Allen White said, "I am not afraid of tomorrow. I have seen yesterday, and I love today." We cannot know this brand of higher happiness until we learn to trust God.

(5) The final step in achieving divine happiness is simply to ask God to bring our lives into perfect harmony with His will, so that we may live as He wants us to live. Most of us want to be happy, but we insist on living according to our own wishes. Of course, that is impossible. The choice is always ours: we can place ourselves in God's hands, or we can refuse.

You and I may be successful if we measure success by a financial standard, but we can never be truly happy until we live our lives according to the commands of God. Someone wrote, "God has never put anyone in a place too small to grow." This is true, but some of us refuse to grow.

Albert Schweitzer, as an accomplished musician, a leading theologian, and a man of wealth, felt the tap of God on his shoulder. He could no longer be happy living as he did. He was determined to give his life for something outside and beyond himself. In *Out of My Life and Thought* he wrote, "I settled with myself that I would consider myself justified in living 'till I was thirty for science and art, in order to devote myself from that time forward to the direct service of humanity."

After Schweitzer's thirtieth birthday he resolved to spend his life in direct human service in Africa. His friends discouraged him; they thought he might even be losing his mind. But Dr. Schweitzer could not experience divine happiness by doing anything else.

Divine happiness is within your reach and mine. In spite of surrounding circumstances, we can be happy if we give ourselves unreservedly to God. Betty Jones lives in Dayton, Ohio. She wrote me a letter after reading a copy of my book . . . *But God Can.* Here is a part of the letter: "Since reading your book, I have turned my life completely over to God, not just half-way. I have cerebral palsy. During the past few years I have had a tendency to become depressed about the few things I cannot do. Now, I am truly grateful to God for the many blessings I have."

We can be happy in spite of poor health, poverty and heavy burdens, if we turn our lives over to God. Jesus called it being "born again" (JOHN 3:3). When we come to know God and catch a glimpse of the truth that life is eternal, when we live according to His will, we will know divine happiness.

3

You Can Bear the Load

THERE ARE many uncertainties in life, but trouble is not one of them. There are many electives in the school called "life," but one of the required courses before graduation is the course called "trouble."

I like to go to the hospital and see the newborn babies. As I look into their faces, many questions come to my mind: Who are your parents? Are they worthy of this sacred trust? Are they Christians? What will your educational opportunities be? To what will you give your life? I never wonder whether or not the child will face trouble, bear heavy loads, encounter the winds of disappointment, or walk through the valleys of sorrow. These are parts of life. The question that gives me concern—the one that determines the destiny of any individual—is this: How will he face the sorrows and bear the burdens of life in such a way that they become steppingstones rather than stumbling blocks?"

Once a sultan commissioned his grand scribe to record a history of the human race. After many years of faithful and laborious work the scribe completed his task and placed five hundred volumes of historic lore on the backs of one hundred donkeys and brought them to the sultan. After one look at the mountain of material, the sultan requested that it be shortened. "Abridge! Abridge!" cried the angry ruler. "Sire, all these volumes," responded the scribe, "may be compressed into a single sentence: 'They were born; they suffered; they died.'" That is another way of saying that suffering is a companion of every life.

I have known many people who have experienced mountains of trouble and sorrow, but I have never known a single person

31

who, after some prayerful thought, would argue that the journey through life was not worth the struggle. For some, the joys of life may be few, but they outweigh by far the mountains of trouble.

I wish I could explain some of the baffling things I see in life. I knew a young man who had loved God through all his childhood days. One day he felt a tap on his shoulder, and heard God whisper in his ear, "I want you to preach!" He responded to this call and prepared himself for the ministry. It took seven long years, after high school, to prepare to become a minister.

After the years of struggle and work, the newly ordained pastor took his first church. But before even one year had passed, it was discovered that he had cancer in one of his vital organs. The physicians told him that there was neither hope nor help from a medical point of view; his case was inoperable. In confidence and trust, the young man committed himself to God and waited. A few months later he passed through the door of death; his brief stay on earth was over. In retrospect, it can be said that that man's life was promising. His influence was captivating; his preaching was persuasive. There is a great need for men like him to live long on the earth. How do you explain it? Who is wise enough to give an answer to such a perplexing tragedy? I know there are pious platitudes and glib answers that one could repeat. But do they really satisfy the gnawing restlessness that we feel within for an answer to why a man's life was spent while he was in his prime?

A young wife stumbles to the grave of her thirty-five-year-old husband. He left her with three small children. There is little bread in the pantry; only enough money in the bank to pay for the funeral; and a small insurance policy. He was a good man. He loved his family. The children need a father. That wife needs her husband. How can this be explained?

Let us look at another situation: Here is a couple who loved God and His church. Their home was blessed with a darling little baby girl. They built their hopes and planned their future around the lassie. Joy, gladness and love could be seen on their

32

faces, and the sun of happiness shone brightly. They laughed, played and sang together. Then, one warm day while the parents sat on the lawn and watched their daughter run and play, the child suddenly fell lifelessly to the ground. They ran to her side, but it did not take an expert to pronounce the awful verdict: she was dead. The parents' hearts were broken, their plans crushed and dreams shattered. I wish I could explain that.

A few weeks ago I called at the home of a lovely woman who is an invalid. For years she has lain in bed and looked at the ceiling and four walls of a tiny room. Before I left, she said, "I don't see why God just doesn't take me home. I am no good to anyone." I thought about her statement and found it difficult to answer. "You just remember this," I finally told her, "God has a plan and you fit into that plan. It may not be easy for us to find our places, but it is our job to keep searching until we find out where God wants us to be, and what He wants us to do."

In view of such baffling questions, we need to review the purpose of life. God is the Source of my existence, and my chief aim is to discover His will for my life and to live it. I am here to become God's servant. The circumstances of life may make it difficult for me to achieve the purpose of my life, but they never make it impossible. God will never ask or expect me to accomplish the impossible.

Several years ago someone sent me a little poem. I do not know the author; therefore, I cannot give proper credit for it. It has become one of my favorite verses, for it has a sound, basic philosophy in it:

> Not now, but in the coming years,
>   It may be in the better land,
> We'll read the meaning of our tears,
>   And there, some time, we'll understand.
> Then trust in God through all the days;
>   Fear not, for He doth hold thy hand:
> Though dark thy way, still sing and praise,
>   Some time, some time, we'll understand.

A few weeks ago I was on an airplane when the pilot informed us that we were going to change our course because of a bad thunderstorm. "This will increase our flying time by twenty-five minutes," said the pilot. The storm caused us to change direction, but it did not change our destination. Life is like that.

I want to have enough money to enjoy a reasonable amount of financial security. I recognize that this is not absolutely essential to God's purpose for my life. I also desire good health. Again, this is not necessary to my living a Christian life. If I had my wish, I would choose not to suffer or bear heavy loads; yet, my wishes do not alter the purpose of life. You and I can live the Christian life in poverty or in wealth, in sickness or in health, bearing the burdens of pain and disappointment or living in the garden of joy and happiness.

Suffering is a part of living. A man would be a fool to believe that he could build a wall around life that would keep away all types of suffering. There is no defense against it. Jesus reminded His disciples: "In the world ye shall have tribulation . . ." (JOHN 16:33).

We must face tribulations in life whether we are prepared or not. I have seen many people buckle under the load of trouble, but I have seen others shoulder their hurts and face life with durable faith and unshakable confidence. Faith in God makes the difference. Jesus walked to the cross unafraid, because of His faith in God. Paul wrote to the Romans, giving them hope in their tribulations: ". . . whatever we may have to go through now is less than nothing compared with the magnificent future God has planned for us" (ROMANS 8:18, PHILLIPS).

What can we cling to during the storms of life? That is a question which all of us need to consider. Amid the uncertainties of life let us think about some of the anchors that keep the ship of life from being washed upon the dangerous rocks that will eventually dash our faith to bits and ruin our lives.

God is aware of the loads we bear. The psalmist said, "For

34

there is not a word in my tongue, but, lo, O Lord, thou knowest it altogether" (PSALMS 139:4). You see, God did not give us life and then leave us to struggle alone. He knows about the burdens we bear.

God knows our sins. The psalmist said, "O God, thou knowest my foolishness; and my sins are not hid from thee" (PSALMS 69: 5). This may not be a comfortable thought, but it is another expression of God's knowledge of man.

One day Jesus called His disciples together and exhorted them to preach the gospel and to fear no man. I think Jesus wanted to impress upon the disciples the divine care of God. He reminded them that two sparrows were worth only a penny. Then He said, "Yet not a single sparrow falls to the ground without your Father's knowledge. . . . the very hairs of your head are all numbered" (MATTHEW 10:29-30, PHILLIPS).

I have always heard that "misery loves company." I doubt the truth of that saying, but even if it is true we must concede that misery is not always comforted by company. I recognize that to understand that God knows when our hearts are burdened is not the kind of help most people want and need. "God knows about my trouble," you may say. "Well that's fine, but what good does it do?" I am the first to agree that perhaps it does not solve the problem or lift the load, but it does serve to remind us that God has not deserted us. He still cares and He is near.

We may stumble and fall, but *God will give us the strength to get up and walk again.* The psalmist said, "My strength is dried up like a potsherd . . ." (PSALMS 22:15). Before life is over, every man comes to a river that is too wide; his leaky little craft can never reach the other side. Every man finds in his path a mountain that is too rugged to climb; his strength is not sufficient to reach the summit. In every life there are rivers that can be crossed and mountains that can be conquered, only by the grace of God. The sooner we find this out, the more pleasant the journey through life will be.

35

I walked into a hospital room a few weeks ago to visit a woman who had lived most of her life according to her own desires rather than by God's will. She lay critically ill and her recovery was in no way assured. When the lamps of earth begin to fade, it is sometimes easier to see the worthy lights of virtuous living. She confessed her sins and said, "I want to live the rest of my life as God wants me to live." She did not know— neither did I know—how much time "the rest of life" would be. I told her God would forgive her past, and I am sure He did. She had stumbled through life, and for the first time in almost three decades she found the strength to get up and walk again—walking as one of God's children.

Paul wrote to the church at Corinth: "Not that we are sufficient of ourselves . . ." (II CORINTHIANS 3:5). Later Paul wrote about his thorn in the flesh. We do not know what the thorn was, but we know it was a heavy burden that Paul had to bear. He reminded the Corinthians that he had made three attempts, through prayer, to have the thorn removed. God did not lift the burden from Paul's life, but He did something that He is willing to do for each of us: He gave Paul the strength to live with his burden. Here is the answer Paul said God gave to his prayer: "My grace is sufficient for thee . . ." (II CORINTHIANS 12:9).

With God's help we can bear the load. On a recent trip to Florida I talked with a woman who was carrying a heavy load. Disappointment, sickness and death had left their marks. "I keep going," she said, "and with God's help I can bear the load."

When life presents what appears to be an impossible mountain to climb, I shall remember Moses. God called Moses to lead the children of Israel out of Egypt. Moses did not think he was prepared; his heart told him that he was doomed to fail, and he made every effort to be relieved of the tremendous task. God does not always give up just because we believe that failure is inevitable. God simply said to Moses, "I will be with thee" (EXODUS 3:12). The same God who led Moses and the Israelites out of Egypt will guide me.

When sickness and sorrow come my way, I shall remember Job. One would have to look a long time to find anyone who suffered more than Job. This little Old Testament man placed his trust in God and faced the storm. Job did not give up; he was determined to bear his load, and with God's help he did. The same God who gave Job the strength to bear his burdens will give me strength to bear mine.

When mental anguish and physical suffering are mine to bear, I shall remember Christ. He prayed in the Garden. He stood before Pilate. He staggered up Calvary's hill with a sure faith. The same God who stood by Christ on the cross will stand by me.

You can fortify yourself against tribulation. While there is no defense against suffering, there can be a victory in it. Paul talks about the Christian armor in his letter to the Ephesians. He advised them to wear the breastplate of righteousness, the helmet of salvation, and the sword of the Spirit. Finally, Paul advised them to pray. One of my favorite verses in the Bible is: ". . . my God shall supply all your needs . . ." (PHILIPPIANS 4:19).

No life is hopelessly lost. A man called me recently and asked whether I would see him. At the moment, I really didn't have time, but he sounded desperate and I told him to come. He drove a five-thousand-dollar automobile and wore a two-hundred-dollar suit. "I have come to the end of the rope," he said. "Unless you can help me, I am ready to call it quits."

After talking with the man for awhile, I told him that no life is ever beyond redemption. "I do not know any magic, and I do not claim any supernatural powers. But I know Someone who can help you. Give your life to God and you will find more joy in the Christian life than you will ever find in your selfish ways. God," I told him, "has a longer rope; why not take hold of it."

37

Remember these things. God knows about the loads we bear. When we stumble, God will give us the strength to get up and walk again. With God's help we can bear the load. No life is hopelessly lost. God's rope is longer than our own; it reaches from our hearts all the way into eternity. Take hold of it.

4

Strength From Above

A FEW WEEKS ago I received a letter from a woman whose adversity seemed almost endless. Her stroke of ill fortune began several years ago when she lost her son in a tragic accident. Then, after a long illness, her husband died. Next, her mother became critically ill and for months the writer of the letter faithfully cared for her. Now, her own health is gone and most of her time is spent either in the hospital or in bed at home. "Why do I have so much to bear?" she asked.

"You have asked a question," I told her, "that has baffled the great minds of all generations. I do not know the answer, but I know Someone who can give you strength, courage, hope and patience—enough of each to help you ride the boisterous waves until you anchor safely in the harbor of God's eternal love—and that Someone is God."

John Greenleaf Whittier wrote ("The Eternal Goodness"):

> I know not what the future hath
> Of marvel or surprise,
> Assured alone that life and death
> His mercy underlies.

Our approach to the inescapable ills of life is important. It is not wise to wait until the storm is upon us in order to determine how we can meet it advantageously. The wise man will weave into the fabric of life some threads that are strong enough to hold life together during days of trouble. We must face the fact that sickness, sorrow and death are inevitable. The question we must ask ourselves is not, "How can I evade trouble?" but, "How can I face trouble with courage and a spirit akin to the spirit of Jesus?"

39

I can become resentful. I can sulk, blame God, become bitter, and give up in defeat. Many people have taken their hurts and disappointments and walked down the road of resentfulness. That is a hard road. You will find no refreshing water of hope or fragrant flowers of joy on such a journey. You will find only the stagnant water of self-pity and the dismal shadows of gloom. I have never known a single person who set the needle on the compass of his soul toward resentfulness and found anything but multiplied misery.

Resentfulness is one way of saying that God is unfair. We begin to substitute our limited knowledge of life for God's infinite wisdom. Now, you would find it pretty difficult to get the resentful person to admit this. The reason is that he has not prayerfully analyzed his hurts in the light of God's true nature, Instead, the resentful person has been living in the jungle of self-pity, crying, "I'm hurt! I'm hurt!" without ever looking or asking for help.

Do you ever feel that life is unfair? I talk with people almost every week who feel that they deserve more than they are getting, even if blessings are coming their way. By the same token, they feel that they are getting more than they deserve if trouble is theirs to bear. If evil deeds constitute the measure of misery one should receive, then Hitler, like most of us, did not receive his share. If goodness is the basis for calculating the years that should be free from ridicule, abuse, suffering and pain, then what did Jesus deserve? When trouble is ours to bear, instead of saying, "I don't deserve this," let us thank God for the strength to bear it.

Resentfulness is also a way of ignoring God. It is not a denial of God; rather, it is choosing to ignore God and walk alone. I was on an airplane recently, and the man who sat next to me expressed the attitude that he did not feel a need for God. He felt that he was completely competent to manage his life, and therefore on Sunday he headed for the golf course instead of the church. He did not deny God, but he chose to ignore Him.

I asked my fellow passenger about himself. I discovered that he was a successful businessman with two small children. There had been no recent deaths or serious sicknesses in his family. He was basking in the sunshine of success and receiving God's richest blessings; yet at the same time he was ignoring God.

"I'm not going to preach a sermon," I told him, "or try to convince you that you need God, but before the journey of life is over, your own inadequate life will convince you that you cannot know true joy and confidence without God." We need God in all of life, in both joy and sorrow; but our need for God is always magnified when trouble descends upon us. We can walk alone, but this does not change God. When you decide to ignore God, you had better be thankful that His nature will never permit Him to ignore you.

I received a Christmas card from a lady in another state last year. About ten years ago I had preached her husband's funeral. His sudden and tragic death cast a depressing cloud of gloom over her life, and she could not master it. She became bitter and resentful. On her Christmas card she penned this note: "I need your prayers. I am trying." That was all she needed to say. I knew that she was making every effort to come out of the resentment she had been cultivating all those years. She had tried to live without God, but no person can ignore Him and know abundant life. She will find her way back; no person ever calls upon God for help, and makes the effort to live in the land of trust, and then fails. The psalmist said, ". . . I found trouble and sorrow. Then called I upon the name of the Lord. . . . I was brought low, and he helped me" (PSALMS 116:3-6). I called; and He helped. This is always the case.

Some people are not resentful when trouble comes, but they sit and brood and ask, "Why? Why did it happen to me?" The question, "Why?" is a natural one. We must frequently admit, however, that we cannot answer it. We are not content simply to say, "It was God's will." Some things happen to us that we cannot attribute to a God of love, mercy and justice.

Christianity is not an explanation of trouble; rather, it is a

41

direction in times of trouble and the assurance of triumph through all of life if we are faithful to God.

Just suppose, when your life is filled with sorrow, that you live in the land of "Why?" You proclaim, "I will not move until God reveals unto me why this thing happened." But suppose your house catches fire? You do not seek a comfortable chair in the living room and ask over and over again, "Why?" You hurry your loved ones to safety, call the fire department, and make every effort to bring the fire under control.

When your child falls and hurts himself, you do not sit down and throw up your hands and frantically ask, "Why?" You take some positive action. You run to the child and try to ease his pain. You call an ambulance and rush him to the hospital, if he seems to be critically hurt. You do all you can to make a better situation out of misfortune.

Christians can take a positive approach. Our lives can be lived successfully in the valleys as well as on the mountain tops. Jesus said, ". . . but be of good cheer; I have overcome the world" (JOHN 16:33).

We can do something other than sit in the land of hopelessness and ask, "Why?" when our burdens are heavy and our strength is weak. Instead of asking God, "Why?" substitute this question: "God, will You show me the way?" When the dark clouds hover over us, it may be difficult to recognize God through the hurt and self-pity, but you may be certain that God is near. The psalmist said, "Thou art near, O Lord . . ." (PSALMS 119:151).

Jesus trusted God, and God's power was always available to Jesus. The cross had a ring of failure about it, and those who stood near it were convinced that Jesus was dead and the Christian movement was over. God saw to it that Jesus was triumphant. By triumphant, I do not mean that Jesus was free from pain. He felt the sting of the heavy whip. His body was sensitive to the sharp nails that pierced His hands and feet, and the thorns which were thrust on His brow brought stabbing pain. What I do mean is that righteousness defeated evil. Jesus

42

was triumphant in the sense that He was faithful to the end and He completed the work He had come to do. The person who anchors his faith in God will never be defeated.

I visited with a hospital patient who had stood at the door of death for several months, barely hanging on to the thread of life. There were days of endless pain, and there was little hope for recovery. I suppose those who passed by his room wondered how he could bear his burdens and how he managed to smile through his pain. It did not take me long to discover his secret. His was a long, hard and painful journey through life, but God held his hand. His daily litany was the words of the psalmist: "My help cometh from the Lord . . ." (PSALMS 121:2).

When trouble descends, instead of asking God, "Explain it! Explain it!" ask Him, "How can I use these tools? The answer to the question, "Why?" can never change the situation; it can only explain the reason. The answer to the question, "How can I use it for good?" will not change the past, but it will direct the future.

There are always two roads which lead away from every experience in life. From each experience we can climb the slope of noble living or we can stumble down into the valley of despair and self-pity. We can weave, out of every experience, a golden thread or a black string. The sculptor can use his hammer to destroy or he can use it to create a masterpiece.

Ella Wheeler Wilcox wrote:

> One ship drives east and another drives west,
>   With the selfsame winds that blow.
> 'Tis the set of the sails
> And not the gales
>   Which tells us the way to go.
>
> Like the winds of the sea are the ways of fate,
>   As we voyage along through life:
> 'Tis the set of a soul
> That decides its goal,
>   And not the calm or the strife.

Jesus could have died a bitter and cynical Man. He could have cried out with His last breath, "The world is cruel and thoughtless!" Instead, He died a Saviour, with a prayer on His lips uttered in behalf of those who crucified Him.

In my early ministry I walked with the parents away from the freshly dug grave of their little boy. The brokenhearted father let his mind span the four years the lad had lived on earth. He was a good boy who loved and smiled and lived every minute of life. As the father thought about his own life, the sins of his past became magnified. We walked slowly, arm in arm, as he began to talk. "I haven't been the man I should have been, but with God's help I will become the man God wants me to become and the man I always wanted my boy to be." That was a dark day in his life, but he walked away from the experience toward the slopes of a better life.

Yes, with God's help, you can be triumphant in days of trouble.

5

Your Life Can Be Changed Through Prayer

"TELL ME," I once asked a friend, "how have you managed to feel so triumphant, even while walking through such dark valleys and facing so many of life's storms?" Before I tell you his answer, let me give you a brief picture of the dark valleys through which he had passed for more than twenty years.

Before the terrible clouds of World War II began to cover the earth, my friend was happy. He had every right to be happy: he was strong and healthy; he had not only a good job, but a loving wife and a fine son. Every Sunday, they made their way to church where they thanked God for His blessings and prayed for the courage to live godly lives.

Then came the day when young John, their only son, entered our armed forces. There were tears and prayers and sad good-byes. John had known the influence of a Christian home, and he knew the difference between right and wrong. His parents were certain that he would remain faithful to both the Christian teachings to which he had been exposed and the example of the Christian life which his parents exemplified. In order to keep their courage high, they talked about the time when the war would be over and their son would return.

The war ended, but young John never returned. He had paid the supreme sacrifice. This, for John's parents, was the beginning of a voyage of trouble, but they managed to hold life together and to live abundantly through their sorrow and loneliness. They were triumphant.

Then, tragedy struck again. The wife of my friend was

45

stricken with a rare disease. The stress and strain of weeks of waiting were hard to bear, and again he prayed and waited. Day after day he sat by his wife's bedside, watching and hoping that she would recover, but the long and faithful vigil came to an end in the early morning hours of a cold winter day. With those he loved most on earth gone, he was left to walk alone. There were days and weeks of loneliness until happy memories brought hot tears of joy to his face. Again, he was triumphant.

Here is my friend's answer to my question: "I do not claim to have been triumphant, but two things have given me strength when I was weak and guided me when my own vision was blurred. First, I have never failed to believe in the goodness of God. Second, I have always prayed."

I have thought about this answer for a long time and I have come to the conclusion that no experience in life can defeat us as long as we believe in the goodness of God and pray for His guidance. We will be hurt, but with these two stones in the foundation of life, we can never be defeated. The psalmist said, "I have set the Lord always before me: because he is at my right hand, I shall not be moved" (PSALMS 16:8). What did the psalmist mean? I think he was giving his affirmation of faith. He believed in the goodness of God, and as a result of God's presence he would remain faithful. He would not yield to temptation; he would face all of life with courage. In simple terms, he was saying that God was all he needed to live the abundant life.

Everyone can pray. God is never impressed with the flowing language some people use in prayer. He scrapes away the superficial and looks into the heart. Genuine prayer is often brief and simple. It may be no more than the following: "O God, help me to be a Christian mother today," or "Grant that I may be at my best," or "Keep me true to the best I know."

Saint Francis of Assisi often sat in prayer for hours without ever uttering a word, except to say, "God." Just sitting in the presence of God and communing with Him is real prayer.

Daily prayer can keep us on the right road. It keeps the line open between God and our frail human spirits. Many of us have never really tapped this great source of energy that is available to us. Frequently we play on the sands of prayer, and sometimes go wading, but most of us have never taken a real plunge into the marvelous sea of prayer.

After attending the funeral of a saintly preacher, I talked to one of his daughters. "He was a good man," I remarked, "and his footprints have been left in the lives of many people." She agreed. "You know," she replied, "Dad and I always understood each other. During his last days I just sat in his room. He didn't feel like talking, so we just sat together. We would look at each other and there was really no need to talk. We understood each other's feelings." That is communion.

There is a classic story of a coal miner named Sam. He had little education, for his schooling had been limited. He had no bank account; his clothes were worn and tattered; and he lived in a little village which, though inhabited chiefly by miners, was a long distance from the working shaft in the mine. Sam walked to work each morning, and back home at night after the long, hard day.

Near Sam's home was a church, and on his way home each night Sam stopped in the church to pray. He was exhausted from the day's work, but never too tired to stop and pray. The minister of the little church had watched Sam go to the altar each evening. Once, as he was about to leave, the minister called, "Sam, I've watched you came to this altar for many months, and I've noticed that you never stay more than a minute. Why are your prayers so short?" Sam dropped his head for a moment and then replied, "Well, I don't have much to say. I just come to the altar and pray, 'God, this is Sam,' and I know God understands."

This story expresses a truth that no Christian would deny. God will never fail us if we are faithful to Him. We can depend upon Him to give us the strength we need in time of trouble.

God will keep us from being afraid if we love and live for Him.

Prayer is *asking*, but it is much more. Paul wrote, ". . . let your requests be made known unto God" (PHILIPPIANS 4:6). Jesus said, ". . . whatsoever ye shall ask in prayer, believing, ye shall receive" (MATTHEW 21:22). Again, Jesus said, "If ye abide in me, and my words abide in you, ye shall ask what ye will, and it shall be done unto you" (JOHN 15:7).

To *ask* implies four things: we ask out of desire; we ask because of need; we ask because we believe God can supply all of our needs; and finally, our asking implies a readiness to receive. I am aware that Jesus said, ". . . your Father knoweth what things ye have need of, before ye ask him" (MATTHEW 6:8). Some people think that this makes prayer unnecessary. But take a closer look at the words of our Lord. He was talking to His disciples; He had just pointed out that the hypocrites love to pray on busy streets where they may be seen of men. Heathens, Jesus warned, use vain repetitions, and they think they will be heard and rewarded because of their long prayers. It is true, Jesus did indicate that God knows our needs before we ask; but He never advised us not to ask. He was warning the disciples not to pray as hypocrites and heathens pray. Everywhere, Jesus encouraged prayer. Asking is a part of prayer, but there is more. We must take the next step if we are to pray as we should.

Prayer is also *listening*. It is one thing to ask God to show us the way, and quite a different thing to wait for God's instructions. I cannot think of anything more immature than to ask a traffic officer for directions and then walk off before he has time to answer. Unfortunately, much of our praying can be compared with this. Most of us do far too much talking when we pray, and too little listening.

Prayer is a mighty spiritual force that can light up the dark places in life. It is present, but it must be turned on before it is useful. Many people live in the dark when they could be

48

living in the light. Before the spiritual light burns in my life, I must turn on the switch by praying. Let me suggest three things that prayer will do for your life and mine.

(1) Prayer will bring God into our daily lives. Once an elderly Christian woman was asked by a cynical skeptic, "Why do you pray?" The saintly old woman replied, "There are three reasons why I pray. First, I am weak. Second, I need God's help. Finally, God helps me when I pray." Those are reasons enough for any mortal to pray.

Before Abraham Lincoln left Springfield to go to Washington for his inauguration, he spoke these thrilling and humble words to his many friends: "I now leave, not knowing when or whether ever I may return, with a task before me greater than that which rested upon Washington. Without the assistance of that Divine Being who ever attended him, I cannot succeed. With that assistance, I cannot fail."

Lincoln expressed a lesson humanity needs to learn. We can have comfort and riches; we can conquer outer space and develop more powerful weapons; we can build great centers of culture and research laboratories; we can clothe the naked, feed the hungry and heal the sick; but without Christian motives and the assistance of God, we will fail. With His aid, we will be triumphant.

The world is full of miserable people who have tried to live without God. Those who try are doomed to failure. Recently a man who has been richly blessed with the bounty of God's good earth sat in my office. Many a man would envy his position. "You are looking at a man," he remarked, "who has unquestionably established the fact that man, regardless of his resources, can never live successfully without God. I have tried diligently and failed miserably." Regardless of our possessions, the fact remains that God is forever and eternally man's greatest need.

(2) Prayer will bring confidence to the distressed mind. I recently talked with a lady who was extremely nervous. She

works in a rather large office with about fifty other people. "I'm so nervous and self-conscious that I find it almost impossible to walk down the aisle to my desk. I dread going to work each morning because of this. I feel that everyone is looking at me and talking about me, and I get dizzy-headed." I told her to use this walk as a prayer trail. "In your mind, picture each person in your office as a friend. Offer a prayer with each step. Pray for each person you pass, and ask God to give you a serene spirit."

Several weeks later the lady called me and said that the best part of the day now is walking down that aisle and talking with God. She has managed, through prayer, to transform a disturbed feeling into peace and confidence.

I have come to the conclusion that the person who can pack his hurts, doubts, disappointments and failures in a bag, and pray about them, will get up and begin life with a fresh start. Real communion with God is our greatest assurance that we do not walk alone.

(3) Prayer will fortify us for life and death. Prayer is a source of strength that will give us confidence in all of life. Prayer will keep the light of hope burning brightly as we enter the experience of death.

The man who communes with God each day is a man with noble and high ideals. I would rather give my trust to the keeping of such a man, even though he may be a poor, uncultured man who lives in a hut and drinks from a tin cup, than to place my trust under the care of one who flouts prayer, even though he may be an intellectual genius whose bank account is bulging and who drinks from a silver goblet.

Jesus was never halted by fears, distracted by bribes or discouraged by weariness. How could He face so much hostility, bitterness and opposition with serenity? The answer is prayer.

The cross looks terribly cruel. It appears, as we contemplate the scene, that the deep hurt in Jesus' heart, as well as the physical suffering, would have been unbearable. Yet Jesus stood before Pilate with an unflinching faith and faced Calvary without bitterness. How could He do it? Again, the answer is prayer.

The same strength that was our Lord's is available to us. We too can face life—and death—unafraid, if we learn to pray as the Master prayed.

6

You Can Talk With God

"*I BELIEVE GOD* is hiding from me," a man said to me recently.

"I know a lot of people who are trying to hide from God," I replied, "but I am certain that God never evades those who seek His help." My friend went on to tell me that in his early life he felt a close relationship with God; his faith was stable and he felt God's presence. "When I prayed," he remarked, "I had an unmistakable feeling that God was near. Now, my prayers seem to fall to the ground."

We must, without apology, concede that there are times in life when faith is strong, life is at its best, and we pray unselfishly; yet God still seems impersonal and far away. Our vision of Him grows dim and the shadows of doubt settle over us. But we cannot live all of life on the peaks of high and holy experience. I do not know a single person who has managed to achieve a state of unclouded spiritual bliss and was able to live there constantly. In every life there are low places. Jesus prayed, "My God, my God, why hast thou forsaken me?" (MATTHEW 27:46). There are, in every life, radiant experiences of joy and gladness, and there are also dark, bitter and perplexing experiences like Gethsemane.

Praying, I tell people, is sometimes like riding a ship through a storm. When the wind blows, the rain falls, the waves beat against the craft, and darkness hides the stars, the captain persistently sails on his course. He cannot see where he is going, but he has faith in the compass. He does not anchor the ship and wait for the morning sun, but presses forward with confidence to reach his destination.

53

When our prayers seem futile and empty, we must keep on praying. Gloom and despair will surely settle over the soul that gives up the practice of prayer. We need to ask God to prepare our hearts for prayer and to teach us how to pray. I advised my friend to keep praying, even though his vision of God was blurred. He will never gain hope and strength by becoming discouraged and giving up the privilege of prayer.

I also recommended that my friend re-use the high moments of his youth when he had felt the presence of God and had left the altar of prayer exhilarated, refreshed and reassured of God's love. "Bring them out of the past," I remarked, "and let them shine a light of faith and trust in the goodness of God on your present path of doubt." C. D. Martin wrote one of my favorite hymns. In one verse he expressed persistent trust in the God who never fails us:

> No matter what may be the test,
> God will take care of you;
> Lean, weary one, upon His breast,
> God will take care of you.

Keep praying, and one day the clouds of doubt will disperse and give way to the warm sunlight of God's presence. Do not be impatient; remember, God is never in a hurry.

I once counseled with a lady who had become bitter because, as she stated it, "God let my mother die." The mother was in her eighties when she passed away. The grief-stricken daughter said, "I prayed and prayed and prayed that God would make her get well, but God let her die." Now, God let that woman die only in the sense that death is inevitable and a part of God's plan for the human family; His will is that one day all of us will experience death, even as we experienced birth. I believe all things are possible with God; He can do anything He wants to do. God could keep us alive on earth and let us live here forever, if He wanted that for us; but He would have to change His entire plan for us. He has something better for those who are dedicated to Him; therefore, He has made death a part of His divine will. We must learn to accept God's will when we pray. Unless we do, we shall certainly walk down a lonely road to despair and come to the land of defeat.

I visited a wonderful old lady who was critically ill. Many of her friends had already made the journey through the valley of death, yet her devotion to the welfare of her children, grandchildren and great-grandchildren made it hard for her to release her grip on life. Therefore, she prayed, "O God, if You have any need for me here, let me get well. Amen." That is unquestionably a saintly prayer.

Prayer is a method of discovering God's will. Dr. Daniel A. Poling said that he prays because he wants God to guide him and help him find the answer to his quest. "I want His answer," asserts Dr. Poling. "Always I may have mine without going to the trouble of prayer."

Dr. Poling described his experience in prayer during the illness and death of his younger brother. He had been called home from out of the city because of the critical illness, and when he saw his brother in the grip of typhoid fever, he said, "I knew what to do." He went into the next room and prayed. His prayer was fervent and sincere. He wanted God to place His healing hand on his brother and make him well again. This prayer gave him no sense of release or satisfaction. He tells us that he was disillusioned; then he became angry, and finally he felt despair. He made demands upon God and pleaded for his brother's recovery.

When darkness came, Dr. Poling took a walk through the countryside. He returned home and went back to his room to pray. He waited, and in utter weariness fell asleep. When dawn came he opened his eyes. "Before I was wide awake, I had my answer. The answer was 'No.'" For the first time, Dr. Poling said, he discovered the secret to that promise: "If ye shall ask any thing in my name, I will do it" (JOHN 14:14). "As I prayed for the recovery of my brother," Dr. Poling continued, "there was no 'thy will be done' anywhere in the wild and anguished cry of my heart. I was ready to settle for nothing less than 'my will be done.' "

Finally, Dr. Poling testified, assurance came with God's answer. "The assurance that 'No' was not only God's word to me, but that it was also the answer I wanted. Yes, it was as final as that. Then I would not have exchanged the 'No' for 'Yes.' " Prayer at its best seeks to discover God's will, and in the final analysis His will is always best. Our task is to learn how to pray, "Thy will be done."

If we want to be happy, we must learn to pray unselfishly. Saint Francis of Assisi mastered this art. Almost eight hundred years ago he prayed, "Lord, make me an instrument of Thy Peace. Where there is hatred, let me sow love. Where there is injury, pardon. Where there is doubt, faith. Where there is despair, hope. Where there is darkness, light. Where there is sadness, joy. O Divine Master, grant that I may not so much seek to be consoled as to console; to be understood, as to understand; to be loved, as to love; for it is in giving that we receive, it is in pardoning that we are pardoned, and it is in dying that we are born to Eternal Life. Amen."

Some people seem to think of prayer in terms of a bargain basement, with tables laden with God's rich blessings. I would be the first to concede that the Christian life is a bargain, regardless of the cost. The fact is that confession, repentance, love and forgiveness are never on sale. God does not reduce the price of these items: it remains the same for all, and the strange and wonderful thing about it is that every man, regardless of his social position or bank account, can confess and repent of his sins and experience God's ceaseless love and forgiveness.

Perhaps we sometimes forget that Jesus was human as well as divine. He did not like to suffer any more than you and I like to experience throbbing pain. His human nature cringed when He caught His first glimpse of the cross. He prayed, "O my Father, if it be possible, let this cup pass from me . . ." (MATTHEW 26:39). This is a clear mark of His humanity. More than anything else, Jesus wanted to obey His Father. His highest aim was to live in such a way as to please God. With God's help He was able to master His own desires. You and I, with God's help, can conquer our fears and subdue our doubts.

Many times when we pray, we are unquestionably upon a battlefield where the principal fighters are God and man. The divine will, wisdom and love of God are pitted against the finite, selfish desires of the human heart. There is a paradox here. Man can leave the arena of prayer, waving his hands like a champion signifying victory. Human freedom makes it possible for him to choose his own way and to ignore God's will. When we insist upon having our way in life, we have not won a victory; we have defeated ourselves.

Two things will inevitably result in utter spiritual defeat. First, the man who refuses to pray will fail. No man can be successful spiritually if he walks alone through the perplexing jungle of life; he must have divine help. Second, those who pray, yet persist in having their own way in life, will finally come to the land of defeat. The reason there is so much anxiety, fear and unrest in our hearts and across the globe is either that we have failed to pray or we have refused to obey the voice of God.

Prayer is one form of cooperating with God. We do not pray in order to change God's purpose. We do not pray in an effort to obtain special favors from Him. We *do* pray in order to discover God's plan for our lives. God knew that He would need man's cooperation in order to execute His plans when He gave man his free will.

The stars move about in their orbits with perfect precision. They never cause God any concern or trouble. The order with which God created His universe is unwavering. The universe has no free will; it cannot think; it has no desires. Man, however, is different. God gave to man a mind and emotions. He

57

can think and choose. Man is probably God's greatest source of joy, but at the same time he is also God's greatest concern. The psalmist, after considering the wonders of God and nature, said, "What is man, that thou art mindful of him?" (PSALMS 8:4). Man is the troublemaker. He is the cause of the lack of harmony in the world. The world's unrest is unquestionable evidence of man's refusal to cooperate with God.

Prayer is often the trigger that releases God's purpose in our lives. God cannot accomplish as much in the life of the man who closes his heart as He can in the life of the person who opens his heart. I like that little chorus written by Harry Clarke:

> Into my heart, Into my heart,
> Come into my heart, Lord Jesus;
> Come in today, Come in to stay,
> Come into my heart, Lord Jesus.

The person who sincerely prays that little prayer every day will experience a richer and fuller life.

The late Phillips Brooks has been acclaimed one of the world's great preachers. His sermons, through the pulpit and printed page, have caused uncounted thousands to turn to God. When God called Phillips Brooks to be a minister, Brooks could have ignored God and gone his own way. It is true that he would never have found happiness in any other work, but the fact remains that he could have refused to respond to the call into the ministry. His life would never have made an indelible impression upon society had he closed his heart to God. In order to use Phillips Brooks, God had to have his cooperation. This is also true with your life and mine. God cannot use us unless we are willing to open our hearts and invite Him in.

The Gospel according to Luke records a beautiful story about a fishing trip. The disciples had fished all night and caught nothing. Jesus said to Simon, "Launch out into the deep, and let down your nets for a draught." Simon began to row the boat toward the deep water. As he rowed, he said, "Master, we have toiled all the night, and have taken nothing: nevertheless at thy word I will let down the net" (LUKE 5:4-5). At our Lord's command, Simon cast the net and it was overrun with fish.

Life is like that. When we obey the commands of our Lord, life is a thrilling journey. When we are willing to say, even in the face of an unreasonable situation, "Nevertheless at Thy Word I will do it," wonderful things will happen in our lives. When God's answer to our prayers seems ridiculous, we must say, "Nevertheless at Thy Word I will accept this answer and believe it is the best, in spite of the fact that it does not fit into my cherished hopes."

We need to pray for God's will to be revealed to us. We are not wise enough to know how to pray as we should; therefore it is important that we ask God to overrule our own judgment and give us, not necessarily the things we desire, but the things we need. Much of the infection of the soul and painful wounds of life are due to the fact that we have had our own way. We have listened to our own answers to prayer, instead of God's answer. The prodigal son found himself impoverished, hungry, and without much character, all because he was given an affirmative answer to his prayer, "Father, give me the portion of goods that falleth to me" (LUKE 15:12). Unless God rules our hearts, we lose our way.

Blaise Pascal prayed, "O Lord, let me not henceforth desire health or life, except to spend them for Thee, with Thee, and in Thee. Thou alone knowest what is good for me; do, therefore, what seemeth to Thee best. Give to me, or take from me; conform my will to Thine; and grant that, with humble and perfect submission, and in holy confidence, I may receive the orders of Thine eternal Providence; and may equally adore all that comes to me from Thee; through Jesus Christ our Lord. Amen."

A letter came a few weeks ago from a lonely man who poured

59

out his heart. His wife and one of their three children were at the point of death. "The doctors," he wrote, "told me that the chance of recovery was very small. I walked down to the little hospital chapel and fell on my knees and prayed. I made some promises to God, and I asked Him to intervene and make them well. By the time I had finished praying, my little girl had entered the Father's house. That was a crushing blow to my faith. I went back and prayed again. This time I prayed earnestly that God would spare my wife to help rear the other children. Just after midnight, death claimed my wife. No one, except those who have walked down such a road, can know the sorrow that was mine to bear. Then," he continued, "God came upon the scene. He assured me that I did not need to walk alone. He took me by the hand and gave me the strength and courage I needed to face the lonely days and weeks and even years that followed." God will do that for each of us.

To pray, "Thy will be done," is to place ourselves at God's disposal. It is nothing short of placing our lives in His hands. We must believe some basic things about God before we can attain such heights in prayer. Let me suggest three:

(1) We must believe that God loves us. No intelligent person can place his life completely in the hands of God unless he firmly believes that God loves him. Love will take away our fears and doubts.

I once talked with a minister who was stricken with cancer of the throat during the prime of his ministry. He underwent surgery and was forced to give up his church. "I am praying," he said, "that God will direct me and show me what He wants me to do. I pray every night that His will might be done. I know God loves me and I am waiting on His instructions."

No person who catches a glimpse of the truth found in the following verse will ever be afraid to pray, "Thy will be done": "For God so loved the world, that he gave his only begotten Son, that whosoever believeth in him should not perish, but have everlasting life" (JOHN 3:16).

60

(2) We must also believe that God takes care of us. God is like a Shepherd who is concerned with one sheep that is lost. He leaves the fold and returns to the wilderness in search of the lost. He is like a Father who grieves when His son goes to the far country. No person can sincerely pray, "Thy will be done," until he comes to know that God cares for each individual.

(3) Finally, we must believe that God's will is always best before we can sincerely pray, "Thy will be done." Unless we believe that God is going to act in our best interests, we will never pray, "Thy will be done." Jesus, in His Sermon on the Mount, said, "If ye then, being evil, know how to give good gifts unto your children, how much more shall your Father which is in heaven give good things to them that ask him?" (MATTHEW 7:11).

Dr. Charles Allen, in *Healing Words*, related the story of a mother who asked her minister to pray for her ailing son. The minister asked, "If you knew it was God's will, would you be willing to let Billy go to heaven?" It was a real tough question, but finally she answered, "Yes." The boy did get well, but there are times when we do not get our way in prayer. We must be willing to accept God's answer and believe that it is best, even though we may not understand it.

When we learn to love God with all our strength, when we learn to trust God completely, when we dedicate ourselves to Him as Jesus did, then we can pray with confidence, "Thy will be done."

7

Steps to a New Life

THE CHRISTIAN church has essentially two functions. First, it seeks to keep people from becoming lost. Second, it tells lost people how to find their way back to God.

I spend a great deal of my time trying to tell people how to find their way back to God. I do not think one could over-emphasize the importance of this phase of a minister's work. There are days when I feel that if we could spend more time keeping people from losing their way, we would need to spend less time directing them back to God.

In our home we are doing everything we can to keep our sons from wandering into the wilderness of immoral living. We prayed for them before they were born; we pray for them and with them every day; we take them to church and do our best to set good examples before them.

What causes people to become lost? There are probably countless reasons, but there are some general patterns that people follow in becoming estranged from God. Let us talk about some of them.

Some lose their way because they follow their desires to be accepted by their fellow men. A hardened criminal in one of our penal institutions, in looking back over his life of crime, remarked, "I suppose I am here not by choice, but because I was willing to do anything the crowd wanted to do."

I talk with some people who are concerned about the cocktail party. "We don't believe it's right to drink," said a woman to me recently, "but unless we do, my husband might lose some of his business and we would certainly lose some of our friends." You see, this is not a matter of wanting to walk away from God, but rather a desire to be accepted socially and to keep certain clients. The end result is always the same, no matter how we lose our way: frustration, confusion, and a sense of meaninglessness within the heart.

Others lose their way because of a distorted sense of values. They forget what is really important in life. Sometimes people live as if they think power is more important than virtue, and money is to be desired over integrity. They grab for those things they believe will make them happy today, and forget that life is not merely a passing pleasure, but an eternal journey.

It was Jesus who cautioned, ". . . lay up for yourselves treasures in heaven, where neither moth nor rust doth corrupt, and where thieves do not break through nor steal" (MATTHEW 6:20).

Still others lose their way through careless drifting. I like to go fishing, and have been fishing in the Saint Johns River in Florida several times. There is one thing I learned on my first trip: one must throw out an anchor or else he will drift downstream. This is true in life. We must throw out the anchors of faith and regular church attendance; we must cultivate habits that keep us close to God; or else we shall find ourselves drifting away.

Then, some lose their way because of stubborn pride. I remember a man who came to see me one day to talk about his confused life. "I am ashamed to come," he said. "I have always thought that I could manage my life without asking for help."

"Don't feel that way," I told him. "No man is completely adequate to manage his life." Unless God guides your life and mine, we shall suddenly find ourselves lost in a sea of confusion.

I have seen many people crawling down the gutters of life, saying with every slip, "I can handle my life." Jesus was the Son of God, but He was not deceived by the thought that He could handle His own life. He was in constant communion with God.

I know a man who was always in trouble. He spent a good many Saturday nights in jail. He was unable to provide his family with their bare needs, not to mention their desires. He liked his "fun." Fun, for him, consisted of gambling, drinking, and spending his money freely on his so-called friends. He lost one job after another because he was not dependable.

For a while I lost track of this man. Then, one day, I met him on the street. He was well dressed and looked like a happy person. There was a glow on his face that expressed something deep within his soul. By the time I asked, "How are you?" he was telling me his story of triumph.

"You know," he began, "I managed my life for almost forty-five years, but now God is directing my life. I made a mess out of living, and I know I'm not perfect now, but life is a lot better since I have placed it under new management."

I talk with an increasing number of people, from all walks of life, who want to know the answer to this question: "Can my life be redeemed?" It never takes me long to answer. The cross speaks so clearly on this issue that it would be difficult for it to be misunderstood. Unless man could be redeemed, the cross would stand as a meaningless tragedy in the history of civilization. The central story of the gospel is that man *can* be saved, and God's power is adequate for all man's needs. God never blocks the road that leads to salvation; if there are obstacles in the way, they are human, not divine. The gospel proclaims unfalteringly and without apology, "Yes, yes, yes, man *can* be saved from his sins!" The only person who is out of reach of salvation is the one who refuses to recognize his sins and who neither feels the need of God's forgiveness nor seeks His mercy. Man must do his part in making something noble out of his life.

"What would you do," asked a young preacher, "if someone came to see you and wanted to know the way to God?"

"That's a good question," I replied, "and I have people in this office almost every week who ask that very question. You can't treat every case alike," I told him. "It's like going to the doctor. There are many diseases. The sick man wants health,

65

but the way to good health may be different for every patient. There are many basic things to keep in mind. Here are a few. A man must believe in God; God cannot save a man unless that man believes. Then, a man must become aware of the fact that his life is out of harmony with God's will. Next, a man must want to be saved from his old habits and evil ways. Then, he must repent and accept God's forgiveness. Finally, he must make every effort to live his life according to the will of God."

"That is essentially what I had in mind," he replied. "I suddenly became aware of the fact that I might possibly influence the destinies of some folks, and I didn't want to give them any bad advice."

One of the most beautiful stories in literature is found in the Bible. It is the story of the prodigal son, and it is filled with both defeat and victory. It is a story about a young man who threw his life on the trash heap and later found his way back to a life of meaning and purpose. In this story we find several basic truths which still serve as guides for those who are lost in the far country. Let me suggest some of them.

The prodigal knew he was lost. There was no question in his mind about his being in the far country. He was among strangers who did not care about his life. It was not long before he noticed that his suit had lost its press and his shoes had lost their shine. Not only were his clothes dirty, but his body had the smell of swine. His hair was twisted and his beard matted with scum. He began to lose weight and he felt the gnawing pains of an empty stomach. He no longer looked like the son of a prosperous man; neither did he act like the son of a wealthy father. We cannot criticize him at this point, because we ourselves do not always act like the children of a rich Father. More often we act like abandoned children, with no one who really loves us.

The prodigal son did not try to fool himself. He acknowledged his condition and returned to his father to confess his errors and to ask forgiveness. So often we play a game of blatant deception. We say to ourselves, "I am really not a bad fellow, compared to others. I am about as good as the next person. I am only following the crowd. Why, the way I live is an accepted pattern of behavior." We soothe our disturbed minds and blur our spiritual vision by standing with the crowd instead of being honest about our transgressions.

A father told me this story about his concern for his son: "For several years I have prayed that my son would be an asset to society. I know that I did not give him a good example when he was young, for I was a drunkard. I suppose he remembers my beating him when I was under the influence. One day a friend talked to me about my drinking. He knew that I was buying liquor with money that I should have used to buy bread and shoes. He also knew that my job was in jeopardy, as well as my health. He didn't say much, but he said all I needed to hear. 'Bill,' he said, 'one of these days your little son will be a grown man. A boy likes to walk in his dad's footsteps. Would you be satisfied if your boy grew up to be the man you are?'

"I went home and prayed. I knelt beside my bed and with my face in my hands I said, 'O God, please, whatever You do, don't let my boy grow up to be like me.' Just at that moment, something said to me, 'Why don't you try to become the man that you would be proud for your son to become?' Since that day I haven't touched a drop of liquor. I have honestly tried to become the man I want my son to become.

"My boy is in college now. One day I paid him a surprise visit. When I walked into his room I thought I smelled whisky. I didn't preach to him, but I told him that I thought it was wrong to drink. 'But Dad,' he replied, 'everybody who is anybody takes a drink.'

" 'There is one lesson I want you to learn,' I told him, 'before it is too late. The crowd can be wrong. I know, because I have stood with the crowd, and I have been as wrong as a man can be.' "

Let us not deceive ourselves. If we are lost in the far country,

67

let us quickly admit it. We may be living up to what is marked "social decorum," and lagging far behind what is genuine Christian behavior. We all know that justice, righteousness and other Christian virtues frequently travel alone.

The men who have stood out in the history of humanity have been those who dared to stand alone. They were lonely and often misunderstood. In one sense of the word, men like Jesus, Socrates, Socinus, Wilberforce, Luther, Wesley, Knox, Lincoln and others stood alone. They refused to deceive themselves, and so must we if spiritual progress is to become evident in our lives. The man who does not have the courage to look at his life and admit to himself and to God, "I am a sinner," will never find his way out of a sinful life.

When the prodigal son "came to himself," things began to happen. He knew that his life was a failure. He also knew that he needed some help. The prodigal looked within. This is perhaps not as easy as it sounds, but it is a necessary step in finding one's way back to spiritual peace from the black despair of the far country. Is it not fair to say that most of us do not make the effort to see life as it really is? We find it much more desirable to look at life as we wish it to be.

Why are we afraid to look within? We are afraid because we know we will not like what we discover. A man from another city came to see me some months ago. He had driven in the pouring rain for almost a hundred miles. As he sat in my office, he was nervous; he twisted his hands and shifted from one side of the chair to the other.

I discovered that he was a good man. I told him that I honestly did not feel that he needed spiritual counsel. I advised him to go to see his medical doctor. At this, I could see tension tighten his face. "How long," I asked, "has it been since you had a physical checkup?" He thought for a moment and replied, "It's been twenty years since I have been in a doctor's office. I'm afraid to go. I'm afraid they will discover cancer!" Many of us are afraid to look within because we may not like what we discover.

Recently one of my good friends came to see me. He had found the courage to take a long look within himself and into his confused life. Before we got started in conversation, he said, "I want you to be completely frank with me. I may be so close to my sins that I can't see them. If you see anything that is wrong, I want you to tell me. I am here to uncover my sins."

It takes a long time to grow a tangle of moral confusion such as that in which some of us live. Frequently, it takes a while to find a way out. But when a man begins to search his life in an effort to see his sins, he is bound to make progress. My friend has not completely found himself at this moment, but he will. As he left my study I bowed my head and prayed. I thanked God that Bill was searching. He is God's man and God will never let him go.

Francis Thompson, the poet, lived only forty-eight years. His father was a successful physician and his one great wish was for his son to become a doctor. As a young man, therefore, Francis went to college to study medicine. He showed little interest in healing broken bodies, however, and three times he failed his examinations.

When he was twenty-six years old he went to London to make his own way. For the next five long years he suffered intense poverty and almost constant illness. Finally, he became a narcotics addict. He spent many nights sleeping on park benches and wrote a few poems on pieces of scrap paper.

Then, some of his friends took Francis into their hearts, and under their influence he found the courage to begin an examination of his life. Following this, Christ came into his life and he became a changed man. In "The Hound of Heaven" he wrote:

> I fled Him, down the nights and down the days;
> I fled Him, down the arches of the years.

Sometimes we must cry, as did the psalmist, "Search me, O God, and know my heart: try me, and know my thoughts" (PSALMS 139:23). We must also do some of the searching.

The prodigal decided he wanted to be somebody. He was tired of living as he did; life had lost its glow. From the watchful care of his father's house the far country had looked like a gay place. He may have felt that he was missing all the fun of living by staying at home.

Now, things were different. The far country had deceived him. The glamour was gone, and the life that promised so much had faded into a nightmare. This is always the case. Evil wears glittering garments, and we find ourselves easily deceived by their false glow.

The prodigal then set a goal for himself. He remembered how much better things had been at home. He thought about the comfortable house. He could picture in his mind the servants, clean clothes, and tables laden with good food. He must have thought about his bed and the love of his family.

The Bible tells us that "he came to himself." Whenever a man comes to himself he always reaches for the highest he knows. In our low moments we may be satisfied with second-rate living, but when we see clearly, we want the best.

While doing graduate work at Boston and Harvard universities, I spent some time one summer in the Bowery in New York City. One night, in the evangelistic service at the Bowery mission, I heard a man tell about his religious experience. He had spent ten years on the Bowery. That is a long time. He looked into the faces of about three hundred men and said, "You think you are defeated. That is absoluetly true. As long as you admit defeat, there is no hope. I've got news for you. God can help you conquer your old habits and He will forgive your sins."

The speaker paused. Then he looked out into the faces of a horde of disappointed men who had failed and said, "I'll tell you how I happened to get off the Bowery. I was tired of being a nobody. I made up my mind that I wanted to be somebody. I promised God that if He would help me I would do my best. God has helped me and I've done my part. You must make up your minds that you want to be somebody and God will see to it that you live a useful life."

S. A. Campbell related a story of Rudyard Kipling. Once, when he was desperately ill and running a high fever, Kipling turned and tossed from one side of his bed to the other. He was heard to mumble some words that no one seemed to understand. Finally, a nurse leaned over him and whispered, "Mr. Kipling, what do you want?" With this, the poet lay still, opened his weary eyes and feebly whispered, "I want God."

I always advise people to set definite goals for themselves. This is what the prodigal son decided to do. I do not know of any person who ever exceeded the goal he had set for himself. If you see a man who is the president of his company, you may be sure that his goal was to become president.

In the Christian life the goals we set for ourselves must be tempered with the spirit of good will. The motive behind our goals must be Christian service. I once heard a group of preachers talking about goals. Someone made this statement about one young minister: "I think he has too much ambition." Someone else said, "I know this fellow pretty well, and he is not so much interested in serving a big city church as he is in reaching a host of people."

Jesus set a goal for Himself. He said, "My food is doing the Will of Him Who sent Me and finishing the work He has given Me" (JOHN 4:34, PHILLIPS). Another translation of this verse might read, "My goal in life is to do the work My Father has given Me." One could linger at the foot of the cross and say with undeniable certainty, "Jesus has achieved His goal." Among our Lord's dying words were these: "It is finished . . ." (JOHN 19:30). I think the Master was saying, "I have reached the goal. I have done to perfection the work My Father sent Me to do."

I remember an occasion when a woman brought her husband to see me. I did not know that he had come under protest until they reached my office. He was a man of great ability, but he

71

was throwing his life away. His wife was making a desperate effort to save their marriage as well as his soul.

It did not take me long to discover that I was wasting the couple's time, as well as my own. Before they left we had prayer, and as the man said goodbye I remarked, "There is not a living soul who can make you spend your life for something good and noble, except yourself. God will never force His way into your heart. You have the only key that will unlock the door and permit Him to enter."

We shall live the rest of our days in the far country unless we, like the prodigal, make up our minds that we want to be somebodies. It is one of the most important steps we can take.

The prodigal son had to get "self" out of the way. This young man was very human—probably not at all different from today's young people who believe they can get along in life without guidance and parental control. It must have been a tremendous mental struggle for the prodigal son to bring himself to the point of forfeiting his pride and admitting that he needed his father. The self-determination which drove him to leave home for the far country had to be buried in humility before the prodigal could return to his father's home.

When news of the death of Sam Rayburn reached the press, many glowing remarks were written about his life. He was truly a great man who served his country with honor. Even Mr. Rayburn's political adversaries had words of praise for him. I have an idea he got a good many chuckles out of the complimentary remarks made by the opposition. I read the newspaper reports with interest, and I believe the greatest compliment paid to Rayburn was not intended as such. It was a sentence buried near the end of one reporter's remarks: "He learned to live with himself."

Just think of it! When a person learns to live with himself he has learned one of the most important lessons in life. What does it mean to live with one's self? It means that one can go to bed at night knowing that he has treated others right, believing that he has done his best, and feeling unafraid of what others might say about him.

The highest mountain in the world is the mountain of self. The prodigal son conquered it. He had already received all of his inheritance from his father; he had no right to ask for anything more. In retrospect, the son looked at his miserable life. His pride had to be overcome. His sins had to be forgiven. Before they could be forgiven he had to admit that he was wrong. He had to ask for another chance. "What will the neighbors think?" he must have said to himself. "What will the servants say? How will my brother react?" These were questions of a wounded pride that had to be overcome.

Finally, as he wrestled with self, he must have thought, "There is only one way back, and that is to admit that I have been wrong and ask my father to forgive me. I must not let myself be influenced by what others think or say. I will swallow my pride and go back home." Then, according to the story, the prodigal said, "I will arise and go to my father, and will say unto him, Father, I have sinned against heaven, and before thee, And am no more worthy to be called thy son: make me as one of thy hired servants" (LUKE 15:18-19).

That took courage! Yet, that was a necessary step in finding the way back home. No one would seriously question this young man's genuineness. He did not ask to live as a son; he asked to serve as a servant. This is how it should be in life. Before we can find God, we must conquer the mountain of self, and we should not ask God's favors unless we are willing to serve Him.

In the account of the funeral of Gerald O'Hara, in *Gone With the Wind*, his prospective son-in-law said, "There warn't nothing that come to him from the outside that could lick him. . . . There ain't nothing from the outside can lick any of us. . . . But that weakness that's in our hearts can lick us in the time it takes to bat your eye."

The fact is that we submit to defeat from within. We are

73

defeated not by outward pressure, but by inner weakness. Little things, such as jealousy, stubbornness, and our unwillingness to admit our sins, will cause us to collapse. Most of us would prefer to hear the voices within rather than to hear the voice of God. This is the greatest obstacle we must overcome.

The prodigal surrendered his life to the wishes of his father; he came back desiring most of all to have a good relationship with him. He did not make any claims on his father; He simply asked for the lowest place in the house. He was willing to be a servant and wait on members of the family.

The cost of the Christian life is absolute surrender. We are never good ambassadors of Christ until He lives in every area of our lives. Complete surrender to God may not always produce the easiest life for you or me, but it will always produce the happiest life. So, if you are looking for an easy life, do not come to Christ because you think your life will be made immune to hardship if you follow Him.

Complete surrender cost Paul many hours of pain: he was cast into prison, he was shipwrecked, he was beaten and stoned, and finally, he was executed. All of this happened because he was dedicated to God, without reservation. Complete surrender cost John Bunyan many years in Bedford jail. It cost Martin Luther many days of ridicule and suffering. It brought Jesus to the Garden, to Pilate's hall, to Calvary where He found a cross and felt the weight of humanity's sin.

Happiness unparalleled will be ours when we come to the place in life where we can say, with Epictetus: "Make use of me for the future as Thou wilt. I am of the same mind; I am one with Thee. I refuse nothing which seems good to Thee. Lead me whither Thou wilt. Clothe me in whatever dress Thou wilt."

Louis Evans, in *Youth Seeks a Master*, tells a story that illustrates God's unwillingness to compromise with our selfish desires and evil ways: "An old Indian chief, in gratitude for his new-found faith and joy, came to the missionary bearing in

74

his hands a pair of beaded moccasins. 'Me give these to Jesus,' he said, proffering them to the missionary. But the missionary, looking at them, shook his head and said, 'No, chief, that is not what Jesus wants.' Bewildered, he took them back to his tepee and this time brought some finely-woven snowshoes. 'No,' said the missionary, 'that is not what Jesus wants.' Finally, the Indian went and secured from the wall of his tepee his most precious treasure—a well-oiled automatic rifle for which he had saved for many years. This he placed in the hands of the missionary, thinking it surely would be accepted; but the missionary handed back the rifle and said, 'No, chief, that is not what Jesus wants.' The old chief stood there bewildered and in abject perplexity, not knowing what to do next. Then, as though a light had dawned, he lifted his eyes to the missionary and said, 'Well, then, me give Jesus poor Indian too.' The missionary replied, 'That is it, chief. It is you yourself He wants, and nothing less will do.' You and I may bring to Christ the finely-beaded moccasins of our service and run errands for Him; we may bring Him the snowshoes of our possessions; we may bring to Him, in utmost faith and belief, the finely-polished rifle of the intellect; but until we say, 'Lord, take poor Indian, too,' and lay our hearts in His hand—the surrender never suffices."

Until a man is ready to meet the demands of our Lord, he can never experience the salvation God offers.

8

Another Chance
Through Forgiveness

A MAN SAID to me only a short time ago, "I would take my life if I had the courage." I urged him to pray for courage to face life, and for guidance to know in what steps God would have him walk as he tries to rebuild his life.

Your life will be miserable unless there is within you a sense of eternal purpose and direction. Most of us are guilty of lowering our sights to the temporary things of earth. For the most part, we seek to satisfy the flippant desires of the mind. We are a generation of people with many desires, and we are ready to satisfy them at almost any price. We want to live in big houses, drive new automobiles, own cottages near a lake, wear fine clothes, have bank accounts, and be accepted by the socially elite.

These desires are not abnormal. They surge to the surface in almost every life. I do not speak against such wishes; if any person wants to give me a new car or build a home on a lake for me, I will gladly accept it. However, cravings such as these must be controlled. If they become our dominant aspirations and order our lives, we have missed the real purpose of life. We must, if we are to be happy, lift our sights from the temporal to the eternal.

Fresh water will quench your thirst today, but tomorrow you will thirst again. Jesus talked to a woman of Samaria as He sat on the curbstone of Jacob's well. He was thirsty and weary. The well was deep and Jesus did not have a bucket with which to draw water. As the woman of Samaria drew some fresh, cool water from the deep well, Jesus asked her for a drink of it. The Samaritan woman was surprised that a Jew would even speak to her, let alone ask her for water. Jesus said to her, "Whosoever drinketh of this water shall thirst again: But whosoever drinketh of the water that I shall give him shall never thirst; but the water that I shall give him shall be in him a well of water springing up into everlasting life" (JOHN 4:13-14). At this, the woman became interested. Water, for her, was a problem; she had to carry it a long way. She must have thought how wonderful it would be to drink from a well that would quench forever the thirst of a parched tongue. She said to Jesus, "Sir, give me this water, that I thirst not, neither come hither to draw" (JOHN 4:15).

The woman of Samaria was thinking about water that would satisfy her physical thirst; Jesus was talking about water that would fill the deep springs of the soul. We must lift our eyes above earthly desires if the deep longings of the soul are to be satisfied.

I talked with a man who appears to be characteristic of a majority of people. He reminded me of a drowning man, grabbing for anything within reach. He was in trouble, and he told me the story of his life. He had been successful in some areas and a miserable failure in others. He had built a wall of selfishness around his life, settling for nothing less than his own way. He left behind him a trail of ugly sins that caused many hearts to break. It was easy to see that he was in a bad situation. I was like a man locked out of a vault in which all the treasures of life were kept, without knowing the combination to the lock. I had to admit that I did not have the key to free him; only God could do that. This is true for many of us. We become so entangled in the evil ways of the world that we are caught in a web. At this point, human wisdom and strength fall short of our needs.

Sometimes I wonder if my sermons are meaningful to those who hear them. For example, I look out from the pulpit and see some persons who are young, and in the prime of life. Some problems are peculiar to youth. Among the congregation there are also older people who face the problems of loneliness, disappointment and fear. Then, I see people seated before me who need a word of comfort and encouragement. Almost every Sunday a few people tell me, "That was just what I needed today." I feel that some others may want to say, "You were not talking to me this morning."

When I preach concerning the idea of forgiveness, I know that not a single person could feel that he was left out or that he did not need the sermon. The need for forgiveness is universal; when a man talks about it, he speaks to all human hearts. The prophet was talking about you and me when he said, "All we like sheep have gone astray; we have turned every one to his own way . . ." (ISAIAH 53:6). Must we not all say, with the psalmist, "I have gone astray like a lost sheep" (PSALMS 119: 176)?

Each time we sin and try to cover it, explain it, or ignore it, we are becoming less sensitive to God, for sin perverts man's sense of judgment. James S. Stewart reminds us that every time a man sins, ". . . he is making himself less capable of realizing what sin is, less likely to recognize that he is a sinner." The only logical conclusion that follows is that he will be less likely to seek God's forgiveness.

David cried, "Against thee, thee only, have I sinned, and done this evil in thy sight . . ." (PSALMS 51:4). The implication here is clear: David had sinned against God, and only God could forgive his sin.

The highways of life are filled with people who are looking for the road which leads to the Father's house. We have all sinned. We have, at one time or another, broken God's heart. He has been disappointed at the way we have faced criticism, failure and sorrow. God, through His Son, has given us an Example of how life ought to be lived. Jesus was kind, generous, forgiving, understanding, and a Man of perfect love. We have

79

been unkind and selfish. We have held old grudges and refused to try to understand. At best, our lives have been tinged with something akin to hate.

I received this letter from a woman: "A young couple married. Soon after the marriage, the husband left and moved to another state with another woman. They lived together as man and wife. After many years they realized their mistake, and stopped having sex relations. Can this couple be saved?" I wrote to the lady, expressing my belief that all people, no matter how deeply their souls are stained, will be forgiven if they repent of their sins.

There is a story in the New Testament about a woman taken in adultery. Some scribes and Pharisees brought her to Jesus, shouting where all could hear, that she had been caught in the act of adultery. She was embarrassed. She was sorry for her sin, and she repented in her heart. The men who brought her wanted Jesus to give them permission to stone her. Jesus would have no part of this. Stoning her would not help. She did not need an executioner; she needed a Saviour.

Jesus did not ask the woman if she had committed adultery; He knew she was guilty. He also knew that she was sorry, and wanted forgiveness. Jesus said, "Neither do I condemn thee. . . ." Her sins had condemned her. ". . . go," said Jesus, "and sin no more" (JOHN 8:11).

Jesus never turned away any person who sincerely confessed and genuinely repented of a sin. God's love, which we see so clearly expressed on the cross, will cover all our sins if we meet God's conditions and accept Christ as our Saviour. Repentance has to do with the past, present and future. We must be sorry for the past, let God move into the center of the present, and give Him permission to direct the future.

How can those guilty of adultery, murder and cheating be saved? These are sometimes called the great sins of the world. True, we should guard against them, but we should also shun the little commonplace sins which are our constant companions.

The majority of us are not likely to become estranged from

God because of murder or stealing; we guard against these. "The things that crucify Christ and wreck the world," wrote James S. Stewart, "are the common sins of every day, self-centeredness, pride, apathy, cynicism, slackness, unkindness, every temptation put in another's path, every wasted opportunity, every pitiful compromise." Are we guilty of these sins? No person could objectively review his or her life and come up with any answer except, "Yes, I am guilty."

I believe Sören Kierkegaard held the key when he said, "I must repent myself back into the family, into the clan, into the race, back to God." There is no time in the Old Testament when God simply patted the sinner on the back and said, "That's all right. You are a nice fellow. Just forget the past." If you think you have heard God say that, you are wrong. That is the approach the devil makes. Jesus never told a person to think positively and forget the past. Repentance is a necessity for the soul who wants forgiveness. Repentance paves the road that leads from greed to generosity, from selfishness to Christian service, from evil to righteousness, and from the dark valley of sin to the bright lights of God's mercy, love and forgiveness.

Over a hundred years ago John Bowring wrote a great hymn about the cross. He described it as "towering o'er the wrecks of time." The cross is God's answer to the heartache caused by evil, and the dreams broken by sin. The cross represents the struggle between good and evil in the world. It stands as a constant reminder that righteousness won the war with evil.

I talk with many people who want to know if they can be forgiven of their sins. One of my seminary professors, who is already in the Father's house, told his classes: "Young men, tell people they can be saved. This is the gospel." There is a great need for this kind of preaching. We have drifted away from God on the barge of indecency and unrespectability. God's lighthouse sends its bright beams of mercy and forgiveness across the black sea of sin. Follow that light, and it will bring you to the harbor of renewed life.

Forgiveness is a two-way street. Before we can be forgiven, we must forgive those who have hurt us. All grudges must be removed from the heart before God's healing power can become effective.

When I was a lad, my father had a narrow escape from death. He was plowing with a tractor one day when he caught his arm and hand between the wheel of the tractor and the plow that was attached. The machinery tore the flesh from his hand. I shall never forget going to the hospital with him. The wounds were a mixture of blood, torn flesh, and dirt. The doctor worked with a gentle heart and a sharp scalpel. "I must clean the wound," he said, "in order to combat infection. A wound must be clean and free from dirt in order to heal." This is one of God's laws, too. Before wounded souls can be healed, they must be free of ill feeling, misunderstanding and hate.

George Herbert wrote, "He who cannot forgive others breaks the bridge over which he himself must pass." Jesus said, "And when you stand praying, if you have a grievance against anyone, forgive him, so that your Father in heaven may forgive you the wrongs you have done" (MARK 11:25, NEB).

Here are five things we ought to remember about God and His forgiveness:

(1) God knows and fully understands the human heart. There have been uncounted millions who have crossed the stage of life; not one of them made an appearance without God's knowledge. He knows more about you and me than we know about ourselves. He remembers every detail about every person who has ever lived.

Jesus said, "But the very hairs of your head are all numbered" (MATTHEW 10:30). Jesus was trying to impress upon His disciples that we are always within the circle of God's care and concern. The psalmist said this about God: ". . . for he knoweth the secrets of the heart" (PSALMS 44:21). There is a line from a song that I like: "His eye is on the sparrow—and I know He watches me."

(2) God wants us to confess and repent of our sins. He is

well aware of our evil thoughts, our neglected vows, our broken promises and our wasted opportunities. We need not make excuses for our sins. Since He knows all about us, it is not necessary to dress the soul in pious garments before we march into His presence. We do not need to arm ourselves with good intentions and noble resolutions.

There is an old song, written by Charlotte Elliott, that always sends chills up my spine. It expresses a great truth:

> Just as I am, Thou wilt receive,
> Wilt welcome, pardon, cleanse, relieve.

Come to God just as you are and He will lift your burden of sin and send you on your way with a new song upon your lips and a new purpose in your heart.

When we confess our sins to God, we ought to be specific. It does not seem sufficient to put all our failures, defeats, mistakes and sins in one big bag and say, "Lord, forgive me." I believe a man ought to confess his sins as he commits them, one at a time.

In *Pilgrim's Progress*, Christian brings a bag full of deeds and thoughts, and places it at the foot of the cross. Then he says, "Lord, here they are and there are hundreds of things I've done and said and thought that hurt you and I've never even seen them to be wrong, but I love you and I want to be your man and serve and help you." You will note that this was the part of his life that he did not recognize to be wrong, but in case he had unconsciously sinned against God, he wanted forgiveness. I believe we could all sleep better if we would confess all the sins we know about and then lay our lives at the foot of the cross and ask God to forgive even the things we do not see to be wrong.

(3) God does not hold the past against us, and His forgiveness is never contingent upon man's future behavior. There may be times when we must take off our coats of pride and stagger

back to the Father's house and say, "I have fallen into the same trap again. I am ashamed. I know I promised never to do it again, but here I am seeking forgiveness." God will forgive. His power to forgive is without limit.

Once Peter asked Jesus, "Lord, how oft shall my brother sin against me, and I forgive him? till seven times? Jesus saith unto him, I say not unto thee, Until seven times: but, Until seventy times seven" (MATTHEW 18:21-22).

Some weeks ago a lady sat in my office and told me about the sins of her husband; he was guilty of many. I told her she would never have peace until she forgave her husband. He had promised to be a better man. She said, "I cannot forgive. I have heard him promise before, and he always breaks his promise."

Suppose God took that attitude toward us? Suppose that after we made the same mistake two, or perhaps three, times God closed the door in our faces? Suppose He said to us, "I'm sorry, I cannot forgive you. You promised Me the last time that you would never do that again"? Thank God, He is not like that! Whenever we repent, God forgives.

(4) Forgiveness needs only to be accepted, not understood. One of the great mysteries and miracles of God is His willingness to forgive.

When David was praising God for the constant love and care man enjoys, he admitted that he did not understand such divine blessings. When I think of forgiveness, I am almost compelled to say with David: "Such knowledge is too wonderful for me; it is high, I cannot attain unto it" (PSALMS 139:6).

An experience can be valid regardless of our ability to perceive and explain it. I use a telephone many times each day. It is complicated; I do not understand how it operates, but I know it works. In the summer I sit in the comfort of an air-conditioned home and read by electric light. I do not understand how electric current cools the house, but I know it works. I do not know how God can forgive my sins, but I know He

84

does. The important thing is not how God forgives, but the fact that He does. There are times when I am amazed that my wife loves me; the important thing is not how she manages to love me, but the fact that she does.

(5) Forgiveness is God's way of saying, "I'll give you another chance. Go back to your task of living, and do better." He gave the woman at the well another chance. He gave Peter, Thomas, and all the other disciples another opportunity to prove their faithfulness.

Dr. A. J. Cronin relates the story of his first assignment in a Welsh town after he finished medical school. His first operation was a tracheotomy on a little girl who was suffering from diphtheria; her throat was filled with mucus. Dr. Cronin took his scalpel, made an incision in the girl's windpipe, and inserted a tube. He instructed the nurse, who had just been graduated from her training course, to watch the girl. If the tube became stopped up, she was to remove it quickly, clean it, and reinsert it. "You'll have plenty of time to do it, and then come and call me," cautioned the doctor.

Before the long night was over, the tube did get stopped up and the nurse panicked. Instead of following Dr. Cronin's instructions, she ran to tell him. "When I got there," wrote the doctor, "the child was dead.

"I was so furiously angry," wrote Cronin, "that I talked to her for twenty minutes, and the next morning I wrote a long report about why she should have her nurse's license taken away and never be allowed to nurse again. I called her in and read it to her.

"I looked at her," continued Cronin, "as she sat there with her face down, chin against her chest, and a little pity stirred in my heart, as she raised her face and looked at me pathetically and pleaded, 'Doctor, give me one more chance.' Tears were awfully close to running down her cheeks, her eyes were full. I turned away and laid the letter down. 'I'll think about it,' I told her.

"All night long in my dreams there came that same quiet, pleading little voice, 'Give me one more chance,' and I waked up and prayed, 'O Jesus, that's what I had to ask you to do one day, Give me one more chance. O God, forgive me for what I nearly did.'" Today, that nurse is superintendent of one of the largest children's hospitals in Great Britain, according to Dr. Cronin.

This human story is typical of the gospel. It is what we need to hear. It is what we want to know. Commit your life to God in this moment. He will forgive your sins and give you another chance.

9

How to Get Rid of Resentment

"*I AM RESENTFUL.* My life is miserable. Can you help me get rid of this heavy load of resentment?" That was the entire content of a letter I received, excluding the address and signature of the writer.

The road called "resentment" is familiar to many people. A pathetic army of them march down this road to despair, defeat and hopeless confusion. Hold on to your resentments, and before many weeks you will find yourself living in the country of chaos, in the state of unhappiness, in the town of bitterness, and on the street of misery.

No person is immune to resentment, any more than he is completely free from temptation. Every person, at one time or another in his life, must deal with it.

In the Old Testament, there is a story about two men who served under Ahasuerus, the Persian king. One of them, Haman, was a foreigner who had managed to elevate himself to the second highest place in the Persian empire, and everyone was commanded to bow in his presence. Mordecai, a Jew, refused to do so. At this, Haman became enraged, and his resentment was so great that he wanted revenge. He built a gallows upon which he intended to hang Mordecai and all the Jews in the kingdom.

Haman's plot was thwarted by Esther, the beautiful queen. Instead of Mordecai going to the gallows, the king ordered Haman to be hanged on the gallows he had prepared for his enemy. Haman was the victim of his own resentments.

That is a parable of those who permit resentments to live in their hearts. We never hurt the person we resent as much as we hurt ourselves. We become the defeated individuals, and our lives lose their glow.

In contrast to this story about Haman, let me tell you another story. It is an ugly drama with a beautiful ending. Joseph was sold by his brothers as a slave to a group of Midianites who took him to Egypt. His brothers committed this hideous deed because they were filled with envy, jealousy and resentment.

There was never any indication of resentment on the part of Joseph. Truly he was a man in whom the Spirit of God lived. Pharaoh said of Joseph: ". . . there is none so discreet and wise as thou art" (GENESIS 41:39). In Egypt, Joseph found favor in the sight of Pharaoh: "Thou shalt be over my house, and according unto thy word shall all my people be ruled: only in the throne will I be greater than thou" (GENESIS 41:40).

During the great famine, men from Canaan came to Egypt to buy corn. Joseph immediately recognized one group of Hebrews as his brothers, and memories began to flood his mind. He remembered the fear that engulfed him the day he was put in the pit and ultimately sold to the Midianites. Still, he had never felt the hot surges of resentment. Joseph's brothers did not recognize him, and he did not reveal his identity.

As we judge fair play and family allegiance, Joseph had every right to harbor resentment. His brothers had been envious and jealous; Joseph had been obedient. His brothers sold him into slavery; they had deceived their father, Jacob. Yet Joseph had only love in his heart for his brothers.

After a while, Joseph revealed himself to his brothers: ". . . I am Joseph your brother, whom ye sold into Egypt" (GENESIS 45:4). The brothers were filled with fear. The sight of Joseph brought ugly memories to their minds. Joseph assured them that he held no grudge, and reminded them that there was no need to be afraid: "I will nourish you, and your little ones. And he comforted them, and spake kindly unto them" (GENESIS 50:21).

What a touching scene! Joseph clearly expressed the forgiving spirit we see in Christ as we meditate upon the events of two thousand years ago when He died on the cross. God's hand was upon Joseph. Even though, through envy, he had been sold by his brothers, and falsely accused by Potiphar's wife, he had never stooped to revenge or resentfulness. He was triumphant through all his troubles.

When we feel resentment growing in our lives, it is time for self-examination. Doctors tell us that it is wise to have a physical examination about every six months; this gives our physicians the advantage of early detection of any disease we may have. We grant the wisdom of this measure, but thinking people know it is also very wise to keep a close watch on one's spiritual growth. Little prejudices and resentments grow. We sometimes cultivate them without realizing it. Let me suggest some questions we ought to consider seriously in this self-examination.

Why am I resentful? You might be surprised to find this a difficult question to answer intelligently. Sometimes we can identify the reason we are resentful, but most of the time we do not really know. We are likely to discover that our resentments are growing out of our own touchy and self-centered lives. Self-pity, a little envy, and a feeling of not being wanted, recognized or loved, will grow giant resentments.

Most of our resentments have no real basis for existence. We sometimes resent those whose achievements are more glowing than our own; it is easy to resent the person who is so radiant that he casts a shadow over our own personalities. Some must guard against resentment when they are in the presence of people who tend to make them feel inferior. Others find resentments growing rapidly when they are around those who disagree with their own views and positions.

Once a woman came to me to talk about her marriage; it seemed to be falling apart. Every word she uttered pointed to a deep-seated resentment she had built up against her husband. This man had a very promising position. He was a young

89

businessman, still near the bottom of the ladder but on his way up; his job was demanding. Both partners to this marriage wanted a better standard of living, and in an effort to get ahead, the young mother got along without household help. She was tied down to housework, and the care of their three active children. She began to cultivate self-pity and looked upon her task as a mother and housewife as pure drudgery.

The husband worked in a nicely-furnished, air-conditioned office, and frequently went out of town for a few days on company business. From his wife's point of view, his work looked glamorous. He came home in the evening well dressed and refreshed. After dinner he played with the children. He seemed to enjoy his work and family.

When I suggested to my visitor that she was resentful toward her husband, she quickly and emphatically denied it. "How could I possibly be resentful," she reasoned, "when I know my husband is working so hard in order that we might enjoy a better life in the future?" She left with an indignant air.

The following day, the young woman called me and wanted to come by and talk with me again. The first words she spoke when she arrived were: "You were right. I got to thinking about what you said, and I discovered my resentments." Once she was able to identify her resentments, she surrendered them to God and she no longer felt that her marriage was crumbling.

What will resentment do to my life? This is another question we ought to ask ourselves during the period of self-examination. Resentments, if permitted to grow, will ruin one's health. If you nurse an injured pride or an inner hurt, it will fester and break down your health. David Seabury wrote, "Experience shows that the pressure of undrained wounded emotion plays a great part in creating fatigue, nervousness and worry. . . ."

Even more serious than breaking down one's health, resentment separates us from God. Therefore, it is impossible to be a Christian and to hold grudges against another. Life becomes empty and our deeds are little more than "sounding brass, or a tinkling cymbal" (I CORINTHIANS 13:1). The reason is obvious. You cannot keep both resentment and love in the human heart.

Jesus, in the Sermon on the Mount, said, "So that if, while you are offering your gift at the altar, you should remember that your brother has something against you, you must leave your gift there before the altar and go away" (MATTHEW 5:23, PHILLIPS). It is useless to pretend that you are a Christian by attending church, offering prayer, and observing religious ceremonies, unless you are also attempting to be reconciled to your brothers. E. Stanley Jones wrote, "The Christian faith teaches that whatever shuts out your brother automatically shuts out your Father."

If you have wronged a person, it is your responsibility to make amends. In this case, Jesus said, "Go" and be reconciled. If your brother has wronged you, it is still your responsibility to make amends. Jesus said, "But if your brother wrongs you, go and have it out with him at once—just between the two of you. If he will listen to you, you have won him back as your brother" (MATTHEW 18:15, PHILLIPS). The Christian, whether he has hurt another or has been hurt by another, is under obligation to make every effort to make things right between himself and his neighbor.

Suppose the other person will not listen to you? You cannot force him to forgive you. In spite of his reaction, if you have done all you can do in an effort to make amends, you have cleared your soul in the presence of God. You cannot force a person to forgive you any more than God will compel you to accept His forgiveness. He does not tell us that we must succeed, but He warns us that we must make the effort.

I receive a lot of mail, some of which is not what you might call complimentary. It would be very easy to answer some of my critics with scathing remarks, but I learned a long time ago that such a response is not in keeping with the Christ who marched unfalteringly up Calvary's hill and permitted evil hands to nail Him to a cross. I have also learned that I cannot afford to harbor resentment if I want to be an effective Christian. Ralph Waldo Emerson wrote, "The dice of God are always loaded. Every secret is told, every crime is punished, every virtue rewarded, every wrong redressed, in silence and certainty. The thief steals from himself. The swindler swindles himself."

What can I do about resentment? This is the third question we should consider. What you and I do about resentment is vastly important. It will mean the difference between happiness and misery. Let us suggest three ways in which we can deal with burning resentment.

We can bottle up our resentment and keep it to ourselves. If this is the course we choose to follow, I can predict with certainty that trouble is ahead. We need to give expression to an emotion as poisonous as resentment; I do not mean simply talking about it, but making every effort to solve it.

I once knew a man who had an infection in his foot. He did not think it was serious, so he ignored it. The infection continued to do its deadly work. The man tried several home remedies, but they didn't help. He then decided to see a doctor. Several specialists were called in and they did everything to save the foot. The man suffered for many weeks and finally the doctors agreed that the only way to save his life was to amputate his foot. Just before the surgeon went to scrub up for the operation, he said to me, "This never should have happened. If he had come to us earlier, we could have treated his foot and saved it."

As the surgeon walked away, I said to myself, "That is a parable of life." We let the poisonous infection of resentment get into our lives and we say to ourselves, "It's not so bad, I'll just let it go." If we bury our resentment, it will struggle for release and will finally erupt in the form of some nervous disorder or organic sickness or chronic unhappiness. Jesus advised us to clear up any disagreement at once: "Agree with thine adversary quickly . . ." (MATTHEW 5:25). I think Jesus meant for us to settle our differences immediately. The longer we

92

wait, the more difficult it becomes. Paul advised, ". . . let not the sun go down upon your wrath" (EPHESIANS 4:26).

Another way to deal with resentment is to seek revenge. This is, of course, an unchristian act; it will bring unhappiness. E. Stanley Jones talks about three levels of life: he calls one the Christian level, where you return good for evil; another he calls the legal or human level, where you return evil for evil; the third is what Jones calls the demonic level, where you return evil for good.

You can never settle a problem by seeking revenge. In addition to the load of resentment, revenge will place guilt upon your soul. Then you will be haunted by your sins until you find God's forgiveness.

Here are two truths you should always keep before you: you will never find a person who is happy because he satisfied his desire for revenge; neither will you find a person who is sorry for his acts of reparation and forgiveness.

Forgiveness and reconciliation are the requirements of God. Someone chided Lincoln once because he had freely forgiven an enemy. "Our business is to get rid of our enemies, isn't it?" asked Lincoln. "Well, I got rid of this one by turning him into a friend through forgiveness."

John Milton wrote, "By taking revenge, a man is but even with his enemy; but in passing over it, he is superior."

Revenge is the soil out of which hate grows. Hate empties the soul of joy, service, happiness and love. It will bring one to desolation. Hate keeps the fires of hell burning bright. No, revenge is not the answer to resentment. There must be another way, and thank God, there is! Gather around Calvary and you will discover the Christian way to deal with resentment.

Some people have carved resentment so deeply in their souls, and it has been there so long, that it appears hopeless. Many of our problems may look hopeless if we view them from our human eyes. I do not believe you and I can free ourselves from resentment any more than we can forgive our own sins. But

93

God has the key. Through Him we can hold that key in our hands. We can, through His grace, free ourselves. Jesus said, to His skeptical and astonished disciples, "With men it is impossible, but not with God: for with God all things are possible" (MARK 10:27).

Look again at Calvary—not a very pretty sight. Jesus stumbles up the rugged slopes to the foot of the cross. On His back we see the stripes; they range from a dark purple to a light pink. He does not flinch. He permits the Roman soldiers to nail Him to the cross without a struggle. He seeks no revenge. He holds no resentment.

Jesus prayed. This is the first thing He did after being nailed to the cross. Not only will prayer guard the door of your heart and keep resentment out, but it will melt all the resentment that you have ever entertained there.

Prayer should be pointed in two directions. First, we ought to pray for ourselves. A person told me once that he thought it was selfish to pray for himself. I agree—some of our prayers shut out a stumbling humanity with their heavy burdens. Our Lord prayed for Himself, yet He never prayed selfishly. Obviously, you and I often pray selfishly, but there is such a thing as cleansing prayer. I am reminded of a line from an old spiritual: "It's not my sister, nor my brother, but it's me, O Lord, standing in the need of prayer." Our prayer of cleansing might be as simple as this: "O God, give me the grace and strength to keep resentment out of my life. Amen."

Second, we ought to pray for the person who has hurt us. It is not easy, yet it is a direct command of our Lord. Think about it! Vengeful, evil men nailed Jesus to the cross. Indifferent men stood near to watch. Some spat on Jesus; others mocked Him. Jesus heard their ugly taunts. What did He do? He prayed! Now, no one has ever treated you and me as badly as He was treated; yet Jesus prayed. How should we react when people hurt us? Without question, we ought to pray.

Can you imagine the surprise of those who stood near the

94

cross? The soldiers were no doubt accustomed to the cries and curses of men being crucified. But this Man prayed! If you want to rid yourself of your resentments and be happy, you must pray for yourself as well as for those whom you resent.

Jesus forgave His persecutors. This is not easy to do. "How," you ask, "can I learn to forgive someone who has deliberately hurt me?" My reply is, "You can't do it alone. You must have the help of God, but God will not fail you. You can forgive." You must forgive, because it is the road you need to travel in order to be saved.

I once talked to a couple whose marriage was in serious difficulty. The husband had been unfaithful. He was sorry; he repented, and wanted to come back to his wife. "I can't forgive him," she said.

"It will be difficult," I replied, "but you must forgive. You must forgive for your own sake. You can never find God's forgiveness until you are willing to forgive." Jesus said, "But if ye do not forgive, neither will your Father which is in heaven forgive your trespasses" (MARK 11:26).

The woman left with a wounded heart, still full of resentment. Several days later she came again to my office. Before she spoke, her face told me about the joy she had found and the healing she had received through forgiveness. "I just wanted you to know," she said, "that I have forgiven, and I know God has forgiven." If you want to be free from resentment, you must forgive those who have hurt you.

Jesus understood those who crucified Him. W. E. Sangster said, "Jesus made allowances for them." It is always hard, if not impossible, to know what is in the minds of others. Jesus said, ". . . they know not what they do" (LUKE 23:34). Could we not make this concession with those who hurt us? It would be better to excuse them than to harbor resentment. Jesus made allowances and then forgave His enemies.

Paul, writing to one of the young churches, revealed in clear terms how Christians should behave one toward another: "Put on therefore, as the elect of God, holy and beloved, bowels of mercies, kindness, humbleness of mind, meekness, longsuffering; Forbearing one another, and forgiving one another, if any man have a quarrel against any: even as Christ forgave you, so also do ye" (COLOSSIANS 3:12-13).

At times there is little room to suggest that we could honestly make allowances. The naked truth is that a lot of the evil in the world is designed and premeditated. We cannot always excuse a person by saying, "He really didn't mean to hurt me." We sometimes sense the fact that the poison dart was deliberately aimed at us. Then, what must we do?

The answer is a simple one, but it is exceedingly difficult to carry it out in practical living. If we are true to our Lord, we must do exactly what He did at every turn of the road. Jesus forgave, and continued to do His Father's will. He knew that holding a single grudge against another would make Him less than what God wanted and expected Him to be.

Not all people know Christ, and many who pretend to march in the Christian army turn out to be cowards. During the hot conflicts of life, we frequently satisfy our selfish feelings, retreat from all that is noble, and leave God out in the cold. It is a gross tragedy that so many wave the flag of the Christian church and so few follow the Master.

Stephen was the first martyr of the Christian faith after our Lord died on the cross. He was ruthlessly murdered. Stephen's awareness of God's love and the spirit of Christ could be seen in his actions as he bore the pounding of jagged rocks hurled by his persecutors. He fell to the ground, his flesh torn and his body pierced with excruciating pain.

It was an ugly scene of mob violence; hate and evil gave the commands. But it was also a grand scene; love was present. Stephen held no resentment. He managed to struggle until he was in a kneeling position and, with his last ounce of energy, prayed, "Lord, lay not this sin to their charge" (ACTS 7:60). Then, his bruised and bleeding body fell lifelessly to the ground.

96

There is only one way to be rid of sin—it will haunt us, burden us, break us, and eventually separate us from God, unless we forgive and find God's forgiveness.

When someone is not as kind as you think he ought to be, why not try to understand him? Ian Maclaren wrote, "Let us be kind to one another, for most of us are fighting a hard battle." We never really know what loads others bear, so let us make allowances and forgive as well as be kind. When we fully understand another, it is likely that we shall find it more difficult to hold a resentment against him. Regardless of his motive, we are still under obligation to forgive an enemy, and we will never be happy until we do.

Prayer, forgiveness and understanding are all wrapped up in one word: "love." Jesus loved His enemies. Evil, hate and indifference stood near the cross. In spite of them, love spoke louder. You cannot have resentment in your heart and at the same time have a heart full of love. You and I cannot cultivate resentment if we diligently seek to follow the Master. If we live in the shadow of the cross, love will choke out our resentments. Fanny J. Crosby wrote:

> Near the cross! O Lamb of God,
> Bring its scenes before me;
> Help me walk from day to day,
> With its shadows o'er me.

Charles Sangster's father watched the Salvation Army in its early days when the Skeleton Army, composed mostly of thugs, tried to break up their public meetings. The thugs threw filth and stones at those participating in the services, sometimes inflicting serious wounds upon them. One day, outside Eagle Tavern on City Road, London, a Salvation Army service was in progress. The preacher was offering Christ to the people when a half-drunken man came out of the public house and knocked the preacher to the ground with one savage blow. The

97

preacher's head hit the curbstone with such force that some thought the blow had killed him. But he staggered to his feet and looked at the brute who had struck him, and said, "God bless you." Then, with great effort, he continued the service. Sangster said, "My Father . . . knew in that moment that the Skeleton Army was defeated, and that these new soldiers of the Cross would march around the world."

We can rid our hearts of resentment if we pray for, forgive, and seek to understand and love others. Then joy and happiness will flood our hearts. That was the mind of Christ. Paul wrote, "Let this mind be in you, which was also in Christ Jesus" (PHILIPPIANS 2:5).

10

The Greatest Thing I Know

"WHAT IS the greatest single thing you know about God?" asked a cynical young college student. I thought about this question for quite a few minutes before I answered. "There are many great things one could say about God, but I believe God's love is the greatest, most perplexing, and most marvelous thing I know," I replied. The love of God remains the most unsearchable, inexhaustible and mysterious characteristic of His divine nature. It would be impossible to explain the life, death and resurrection of Jesus, aside from this love. Without recognizing God's love, we could not attempt to analyze intelligently His unfaltering concern, unfailing care, and limitless ability to forgive, which we find so evident in life.

If I knew that I had only one more sermon to preach, I do not think it would be a problem for me to select a subject. I would choose to discuss "God's Love for an Undeserving Humanity." We live in a time when there seems to be a general disregard for one another and a prevalence of sheer ignorance of divine laws and the love of God. People need to be told about God's love.

Here is a letter which is typical of much of my mail: "What can I do for a flagging faith? Sometimes I believe in nothing at all; then, there are other times when I really do believe in a Supreme Being. Still, there are other times when I believe in God but not in His impartiality. I am fifty-eight years old and a complete failure. When I look back on my life, I see nothing but mistakes."

Everything I know about the Christian faith is based on God's love. He forgives us, not because we merit forgiveness, but because He loves us. He has made it possible for us to live abundantly as a result of His love.

Unfortunately, in our English language the word "love" expresses several different meanings. We use the word to describe everything from affection between the sexes to the deepest expressions of man's appreciation for God. In the Greek language, however, there are several words which are interpreted "love" in English. *Eros* is one of these Greek words. It means erotic or physical love; basically, it is love in a selfish form. *Philia* is another Greek word which we translate into English as "love." It denotes friendship, or brotherly love. Then, *agape* is still another word which the Greeks use to express love. This is a much deeper type of love; it is universal and unselfish.

Jesus always used *agape* when He was talking about love. We get a blurred meaning of the teachings of Jesus when we try to think of love only in terms of mutual affection or a liking for a person. Jesus said, "Thou shalt love thy neighbour as thyself" (MATTHEW 19:19). It is obvious that in this interpretation one's neighbor is not confined to the amiable person next door or the one down the street who lends us his car, trims our lawn while we are on vacation, or invites us to his home for a steak dinner occasionally. The word "neighbor" includes the fellow who is not at all congenial. He may have a sulky disposition. He may live next door or across the seas. Regardless of his lack of congenial and pleasing personality traits, we are commanded by Jesus to love our neighbor, and the insolent fellow, too, is our neighbor.

As the Greek word *agape* is translated, it corresponds with our interpretation of Christian love. It is the way God intends for us to love others. It is the giving of self, unhesitatingly, unconditionally, and without limit. This love seeks and wishes for others the highest possible good. Christian love desires for all humanity a good relationship with God.

Within the last few decades, men have talked about orbiting the earth. This was little more than science-fiction until a few years ago. Admittedly, I stood for a time in the army of skeptics; I just could not make myself believe that such a feat was possible. Now, history will never let us forget the day John Glenn made his historic flight around the earth.

On that day, I caught a plane to fulfill a speaking commitment in another state. On the plane, the pilot gave his passengers radioed reports as Glenn orbited the earth, then reported his descent into the Atlantic Ocean. As I thought about it, the space flight was still a mystery, and I did not understand it, but I could no longer deny it or stand with the skeptics.

God's wonderful love is as real as space pioneering. It remains a deep mystery, but I cannot deny it. The sensitive soul can see evidence of God's love everywhere in the world. I have seen such evidence in the skillful hands of a surgeon and in the serving hands of a kind and patient nurse. I have felt the presence of God's love as I held an infant close to my heart. I have heard the evidence of God's love in the voice of a minister who spoke kindly to one whose aim seemed to be to injure another. Yes, God's love is here. It can be ignored, but it can never be destroyed. I have seen it expressed in the eyes of little children as well as in the words and deeds of mature persons.

Our minds cannot fathom the depth of the love of God. Every time I think of the cross I am reminded of God's love for me, and many questions come to my mind. Why did He love me so much? Why was He willing to pay such a high price for me? How can I ever express my appreciation for His love? I do not have an answer to these baffling questions.

I want to suggest five things about divine love which we should never lose sight of as we travel down the road of life. Remembering and believing these affirmations about God's love will sustain us through sickness and pain, shelter us in every storm, reassure us as we struggle through the valley of bitter sorrow, and keep the light of faith burning brightly when the way is steep and disappointment and despair are near.

101

(1) Divine love is magnetic. It pulls us toward that which is honorable and noble. God invites us to desert our allegiance to selfishness and retreat from our place of evil, and to live in His love. There is within each of us a restless longing for God. We can never be truly happy until we give ourselves to Him. St. Augustine expressed this idea many centuries ago. He asserted that we are made for God and are restless until we find rest in God.

When I was the pastor of the University Methodist Church in Havana, Cuba, a young university student asked to see me at the conclusion of one of our morning worship services. I asked him to meet me in the study so that as soon as I had greeted those who were leaving the church I could talk to him. He told me about his early life. His parents never went to church; they did not even believe in God. "I am restless," he said, "and my life has little purpose beyond graduating from law school, finding a suitable wife, and living a comfortable life. I have been searching for something, and as I sat listening to your sermon this morning, I suddenly became aware of the presence of God. I want to know this God of love about whom you preached. I believe God is my greatest need." We talked and prayed together, and in the quietness of my study he let God come into his heart.

I never quite feel adequate to preach the gospel. Every time I mount the pulpit I pray that God will take my feeble efforts and magnify and use them to draw men, women, boys and girls closer to His will for their lives. In Havana, God took that sermon, poor as it was, and His magnetic love drew a lost student to discover for the first time His forgiveness and compassion.

Calvary is earth's greatest breach with justice, but at the same time it is our clearest picture of God's love. One cannot, with the marvel of mind and imagination, travel back across the centuries and stand at the foot of the cross and look afresh upon that scene without being drawn closer to God. His love will never desert us; it will always see us safely through the dark nights as we journey toward the door that leads to the living room of God.

The centurion, who was probably in charge of the crucifixion, watched Jesus as He was nailed to the cross. In his official capacity, he had witnessed many crucifixions, but this Man, Jesus, was different from all the other victims. The spirit and courage of Jesus captivated the man's mind and imagination, and he probably never took his eyes off Him during His long ordeal. At the beginning of the crucifixion, the centurion must have shared the common view of others that Jesus was a criminal and that His execution was evidence of His guilt.

God's magnetic love, as expressed in Jesus as He suffered on the cross, drew the Roman officer toward God. When Jesus died, I suspect that the centurion was the first man to speak. Without being conscious of the crowd around him, he said, "Truly this man was the Son of God" (MARK 15:39).

Some men have speculated that the centurion's remark may have been a bit of bitter sarcasm; Jesus, who claimed to be the Son of God, the King of the Jews, died helplessly on the cross. Others have fostered the idea that the centurion meant that He was worthy to be numbered among the many Roman gods. I believe that this man, for the first time in his life, felt the magnetic force of God's love pulling him out of his pagan world of hate into the Christian world of love and service.

(2) There is in God's love a strange, transforming power. It is through God's love that we are forgiven of our sins and cleansed from the stains of evil thoughts and deeds. In the First Epistle of John we read, "Beloved, let us love one another: for love is of God; and every one that loveth is born of God, and knoweth God. He that loveth not knoweth not God; for God is love" (1 JOHN 4:7-8).

I do not deny the good we see in many people, but neither can I be blinded to the evil in our world. Our society is swimming in a cesspool of filth and evil. We have come to the place where, all too frequently, we accept as right and true that which the majority views as honorable. Often, the moral standard is no higher than our desires. I have heard people say, "A thing is not wrong unless you get caught." How absurd can they be! An evil act concealed is just as wrong as one the entire world can see!

Our only hope is to get back in our places and let God be God. We are sinners who stand in need of God's grace. We cannot redeem ourselves. We cannot be happy, or know inner peace, or feel any sense of spiritual satisfaction until we are transformed by the love of God. Let us never forget that God's love made the abundant life possible for all of us. No one is excluded. Jesus died for all humanity.

(3) God's love is personal. I talk with people occasionally who feel that they have been deserted and forsaken. Our friends may be unfaithful to us, but God's love is both ceaseless and unchanging. The psalmist felt that God had forsaken him, and Jesus repeated the same phrase as He hung on the cross: "My God, my God, why hast thou forsaken me?" (PSALMS 22:1; MARK 15:34). There are times in almost every life when a person feels lonely and deserted. But when life is over I believe we shall all say with the psalmist: "The Lord hath been mindful of us . . ." (PSALMS 115:12). David, in his old age, wrote, "I have been young, and now am old; yet have I not seen the righteous forsaken . . ." (PSALMS 37:25).

A man came to my home to see me one stormy night. He talked about taking his own life. He felt alone in the world, for his wife had deserted him and his children had turned against him. He sat like a piece of stone. Outside, the lightning flashed, the thunder roared and rain pelted against the windowpane. My visitor stared out into the storm. "I have always believed in God," he said, "but the way I feel tonight, I don't believe God knows that I even exist. I feel like one of those drops of rain, lost in a cruel, dark world where no one loves me or cares for me." He paused, and for a few minutes we sat in complete silence. I did not speak, because I did not believe that he had finished. "Do you believe," he continued, "that God really loves me?"

I remembered that in a previous interview with the man he had told me about his wonderful mother and her constant love and care for her nine children. She had already gone to her eternal reward. "Before I answer your question," I replied, "I want us to pray, and then I want to ask you two questions." We prayed.

"Do you believe that your mother loved you?" was my first question. "Yes," he replied. I reminded him that he was a member of rather a large family, but his mother was able to love each and every one of her children. I once knew a woman who had twenty-one children, and every one of them knew, beyond the shadow of a doubt, that his mother loved him with all her heart. God's love is great enough for each child to have all he wants.

"Do you believe that Jesus Christ gave us a clear picture of the Father?" was my second question. He unhesitatingly replied, "Yes." That man walked out into the storm-battered night with a renewed sense of God's love.

My mother has four sons and one daughter. She has loved, still loves, and will love us throughout eternity. I feel certain that we have all been sources of concern for her and she has lost many hours of sleep when we were away from home at night. I have heard her say many times, "I just can't go to sleep until the last one is home and in bed." I have often felt that my mother's love is very much like God's love.

Jesus told us a very beautiful story once which gives us additional insight into God's unbounded love for each one of us. A good shepherd thinks of the safety of all of his sheep. He leaves those which are safely bedded down for the night and heads back to the rugged hills in search of the one which is lost. When the shepherd finds the stray, he tenderly places it on his shoulders and carries it to safety. God never created a person who will be dwarfed because there is not enough of His love to go around. God is great enough to take care of His universe and, at the same time, to give to each of us all the attention we need.

(4) God's love is eternal. His love never gives us up; it follows us up and down the road of life. We can refuse to accept God's love, and if we do, I venture to say that it follows us even down the corridors of hell. When God made us, He showered us with love, and nothing can change, alter or stop that love. Paul wrote, "For I am persuaded, that neither death, nor life, nor angels, nor principalities, nor powers, nor things present, nor things to come, Nor height, nor depth, nor any other creature, shall be able to separate us from the love of God, which is in Christ Jesus our Lord" (ROMANS 8:38-39).

I remember reading in a newspaper, several years ago, an account of a wayward son. For years he had been a source of trouble, embarrassment and sorrow to his father. After being involved in serious trouble, he left home and for years his father did not hear from him. He kept waiting and hoping that his son would come back and face the penalty for his crime. The father grew weary with the years, but his love grew stronger. Finally, the boy, by then a man, was involved in an automobile accident and the publicity from that event led to the discovery that he was a "wanted man" in his home state. He was brought back to his native town to stand trial, and some newspaper reporters went to talk to his father.

"How do you feel about your son?" a reporter asked.

"He's my son," the old man replied. "I am ashamed of what he has done, but I love him and I forgive him. I plan to stand by him until the end."

As I read that father's statement, I said to myself, "That is like my father's love and my heavenly Father's love. I am certain that God looks down with pity and sees us moving in our little worlds of selfishness and greed. He knows all about our ugly deeds; we are criminals in His sight. I believe He is con-

106

stantly saying, "They are my sons and daughters. I am ashamed of the way they live, but I love them and I am willing to forgive them. I will stand by them until the end."

It would be impossible to measure God's love for us, but we know that He loved us enough to give His only Son to die on Calvary for our sins. Men mocked our Lord, spat on Him, pressed a crown of thorns on His head, drove great nails through His hands and feet, and watched Him die. In spite of this, His love flowed freely to those who crucified Him.

I feel humble when I think of such marvelous love. I do not merit God's love, but I accept it gladly and, I sincerely hope, with a grateful heart. Never say to yourself, "No one loves me." God's love is higher than the mountain of our selfishness, deeper than the ocean of our sins, and wider than our indifference to all that is noble and sacred.

(5) God's love will triumph. We are not fighting a losing battle. I know that the stories in our daily newspapers present a rather gloomy picture of humanity. Hate, suspicion, fear and misunderstanding are well dressed. The infection of corruption seems to have penetrated government, labor and industry. Cheating, infidelity and gratification of selfish desires are evident everywhere. This country's finest young men and women have gone to the battlefield more than once to preserve freedom and assure peace. The person who is forty years old today has never lived in a world where peace looked secure. It is constantly threatened.

Communism, a philosophy that denies the existence of God, has made gigantic strides within recent decades. In spite of the evil that is evident in our world, the Christian faith continues to proclaim that love will win; God will not be defeated. You cannot condense the plans and power of God and neatly place them in the framework of man's limited logic. Jesus said, ". . . but with God all things are possible" (MATTHEW 19:26).

One day the tyrants of hate will be silent, the legions of evil will have surrendered to love, and God will rule supreme. God wants to triumph through the human soul. His Kingdom could be established if we would be obedient to Him. But God's success does not hinge on the human heart. God would be glad for man's cooperation, and I believe He wants man to share in this victory, but with or without man, God's love will triumph.

No person will ever be able to convince me that God would invest so much in humanity if He did not intend to win. God has always been assured of victory. He would not have exposed His Son to a sinful and undeserving humanity, nor would He have permitted His Son to suffer anguish in the Garden and agony on the cross, had He not been assured of triumph.

11

Love Stands Battered but Unbeaten

I ASKED a group of young people the following question: "Where is the loneliest place in the world?" Some suggested the parched desert, others the rugged mountains where men have never set foot, and still others the middle of the restless ocean. Then, one boy turned to me and said, "Give us your idea."

"The loneliest place in the world," I replied, "is the human heart when love is absent." Where there is no love, there is desolation, emptiness and loneliness that defy description. One can be surrounded with people and luxury, and still be lonely. Some of the loneliest people I know live in the midst of rushing crowds in great metropolitan cities.

I talked to a person some time ago who is healthy, rich and well educated. Many people, who could have no way of reading the message of this man's heart, might envy his place in life. In another encounter recently, this man expressed the feeling that life is not worth the struggle, and that suicide appears to be the only answer. He has money, position and health, but he lacks love.

Human nature is the same everywhere. People need to love and be loved. We see evidence of this basic need in our magazines. We see it clearly on the front page of almost every newspaper. It colors our literature. We even find it in music—from hillbilly to opera or opera to hillbilly, depending upon where you stand. There is a line in one song that I remember from my youth: "You ain't living until you're loving."

While preaching a series of sermons in another state, I was driven around a city one day by an outstanding member of the church in which I was preaching. This man was also an outstanding citizen of the community. As we drove through a beautiful residential section he pointed to one of the loveliest houses I have ever seen. "The man who lives there is the richest man in our city," he said, "He owns more property and probably has more income than any two other men here." I am always interested in where people go to church; therefore, I asked, "Where do they attend church?"

"That's just it," he replied, "they have not been inside a church in twenty years. They have one son who is a drunkard, and another son in prison. There is more hell and misery inside that house than any other place in this city." That story is repeated, to some degree, over and over in every city in America. Where love is absent, misery, despair and loneliness live in abundance.

I remember when my sister, three brothers and I were still at home with my parents. We always had enough to eat, but there were times when we were a bit short on sugar. One thing that stands out in my memory is that we were never short on love. There was plenty of it to go around and I was not aware that we did not have all the money in the world until I was approaching my teen years.

My mother and father believed, with Harold Hulbert, that "Children need love, especially when they do not deserve it." I can truthfully say that my childhood is a book of golden memories, not because we children were showered with things that money could buy, because that would not represent the whole truth, but because my mother and father gave us the things you cannot buy with all the money in the world. I do not mean to say that we went without our share of toys; I got far more than I deserved. But love was the cornerstone of our house. Our parents taught us to love each other, to love God, and to forgive each other. Finances may have been shaky, but the foundation of love never once trembled.

Love is the ladder one must climb in order to achieve any noble goal; it is necessary for survival. Without love we may exist for a while, but we can never survive for long. Love is also necessary for our happiness. People search for happiness in sports, vice, hobbies—all sorts of recreation. It cannot be found in any of these. Happiness is found in Christian love. Love is also necessary for our fulfillment. Without love, you and I can never become what God wants us to become. God made us to love Him and to love each other: "Thou shalt love the Lord thy God with all thy heart, and with all thy soul, and with all thy mind. This is the first and great commandment. And the second is like unto it, Thou shalt love thy neighbour as thyself" (MATTHEW 22:37-39). We shall never find inner peace and satisfaction until Christian love becomes the center of our lives. God made us that way.

No virtue is placed above that of Christian love. It is the basis of all other goodness. Paul emphasized the importance of love in his first letter to the Corinthians. He stated with amazing clarity that one might speak with the combined eloquence "of men and of angels" (13:1), but without love such eloquent speech is useless. Even if one possessed the marvelous gift of foretelling the future and knew the secrets of God, these cherished gifts, without love, would avail nothing (13:2). One might have a perfect faith and, to satisfy his convictions, sell all earthly possessions to feed the hungry, and even allow his body to be burned; but unless love is present, even then, he would achieve precisely nothing (13:3). Paul was saying that unless life is rooted in love, all our efforts are in vain. We may achieve fame, but without love we can never reach our destinies.

There are those who feel that if you provide children with good food to eat, clean clothes to wear, a nice place to live, and expose them to all the cultural advantages, they will automatically grow up to be good citizens. Of course, that is a misconception. The greatest need of a child is to feel the security which is demonstrated in love. You can give children everything in the world that money can buy, but if you fail to give them love you have failed miserably as parents. Our first responsibility

111

as parents is to make a sustained effort to meet the basic needs of our children. This means we must feed and clothe them, but it also means that we must love them and teach them to love. Jesus said, "But whoso shall offend one of these little ones which believe in me, it were better for him that a millstone were hanged about his neck, and that he were drowned in the depth of the sea" (MATTHEW 18:6). If we fail to love our children, we do them immeasurable harm.

Let me tell you a story of which I am deeply ashamed. When I was a lad, a classmate persuaded me to run away from home with him. I left without extra clothing or money and, of course, without the knowledge or permission of my family. We hitchhiked to another city and spent the long night in a bus terminal. The next day we headed for home. Just one night when a youngster is away from home can be a long time for anxious parents. It can also be a long time for a lad who knows he has done wrong.

To place the unnecessary burden of worry upon my parents was the most unkind thing I ever did to them. I scarcely knew what to expect when I reached home. I thought such behavior would demand a good thrashing. I knew one question that my Dad would ask: "Why did you run away?" so I made up what I thought was an answer that might place me in the light of mercy rather than justice. My father asked the question I expected. I replied, "I left home because I didn't feel that you loved me." Of course, that was a lie. I knew they loved me.

I did not receive the punishment that I rightly deserved. Instead of a good thrashing, my parents took me to my room and prayed for me and talked to me. They did not actually make me afraid to run away again, but they gave me a feeling that ought to make any boy want to stay at home as long as possible. I shall never forget that late afternoon. The shadows were lengthening and darkness approached. My mother and father put their arms around me and, with tears streaming down their cheeks, said, "Son, you have caused us a lot of worry, but we love you with all our hearts and we shall always love you. We want you to stay home and be a happy member of our family." That was almost twenty-five years ago, and that ugly, thoughtless behavior has not been mentioned in my family since. I realized in that moment that the love of my parents was unfailing. I have never slept quite as securely as I did that night. I did not deserve such love, but then, we never deserve love. It is always a gift.

Instead of running away from home because no one loved me, I knew I was leaving those who loved me most. Life is like that. God has a mighty big family and many of His children are disobedient. They leave home, perhaps because of the feeling that no one really loves them. The truth is, when they run away from God, they are leaving the one Person who loves them most. When they come back to God, they will find that they do not get what they deserve. The Father will receive them gladly and He will assure them of His love and forgiveness. They will also hear Him whisper, "I shall always love you and I want you to stay home and be a happy member of our family."

Everywhere in the life of Jesus we see clearly the evidence of His love. He never turned anyone away. His love surrounded all who came His way—the leaders of the synagogue, the sick, the troubled and the outcast. Once Jesus said, "As the Father hath loved me, so have I loved you: continue ye in my love" (JOHN 15:9). Jesus indicated in these unmistakable terms that His love toward us is like God's love, and we are to love others as God loves us. "Love one another" is a phrase that Jesus used on several occasions.

When Randall, our older son, was four years old he asked for permission to go somewhere against which my best judgment rebelled. I told him he could not go. In his bitter disappointment he said, "I don't love you any more!" I pulled him onto my lap and asked, "Why don't you love Daddy any more?" He looked up and without hesitation replied, "Because you won't let me go."

I turned his little head toward mine and said, "I want you

113

to remember one thing as long as you live: I love you, and no matter what you do or how you feel toward me, I will always love you. I hope you won't ever do anything that will cause me shame or hurt your mother, but remember that I love you and nothing can change that love." By this time he had his arms around my neck and he said, "I really do love you, Daddy."

If God does not give us our way, we are like little children and we say, by our attitudes and the way we live, "I don't love You any more, God!" If we are sensitive to the voice of God we hear Him say over and over again, "I love you and I shall always love you. My love never changes."

We would do well to look within, periodically, and check on our motives for loving God. Do we love Him because of His marvelous gifts? Do we love Him because we feel that to do so will bring us extra privileges? Or do we love Him because of Himself? If our love for God is based on His gifts to us, then we do not really love God; we simply love the gifts He gives. To love God as we should, we must pray, with one of the saints, "O God, it is Thee I crave, and not Thy gifts."

I like John Bowring's hymn about the cross. I do not wish to do this great hymn an injustice by changing it, but the second verse will better express some of my feelings about the love of God if I substitute the words "God's love" for the words "the cross":

> When the woes of life o'ertake me,
> Hopes deceive, and fears annoy,
> Never shall God's love forsake me:
> Lo! it glows with peace and joy.

Once a little four-year-old girl was told by her stern parent, "Eat your peas!" The little girl responded, "I don't like peas." Her father remonstrated, "You eat your peas or leave this table immediately!" The little girl was crushed with hurt as she left the table. Her father followed shortly after to see what she was doing. He found her looking at herself in a mirror, tears streaming down her cheeks, and singing, "Jesus Loves Me." There is one thing that the birth, life and death of Jesus make clear to us, and that is the fact that God loves us.

Some time ago, while making pastoral calls, I discovered a thrilling story in which two of my good friends shared. John Ryan, a busy, successful, young executive was playing with his children in his backyard. His lovely wife Jean, upon answering the front doorbell, found a little, skinny, thin-faced, long-haired boy standing at the door. His clothes were clean but ragged. "I wanted to know if you need any pine needles today," he asked politely. Jean called to her husband, "John, do we need any pine needles?" Unaware of the needy-appearing lad, John replied without hesitation, "No."

The boy walked slowly away, but Jean could not get him off her mind. A few minutes later, when John and their youngsters walked into the den, Jean mentioned the little boy. He had seemed so nice. "Which way did he go?" inquired John. "I think he went down the street," Jean answered.

John Ryan jumped into his car and drove up and down the streets in the neighborhood until he found the boy. He drove up beside him and said, "Sonny, you were at my house a short time ago, selling pine needles. We didn't need any." He quickly rolled some bills and placed the money in the lad's hand. "Here's some money that I would like to give you for being so nice and polite." The little boy's eyes brightened and a big smile came across his face as he said, "Thank you, sir." John, barely able to keep back the tears, quickly drove away. His compassion was love in action. It was a simple act, but I am certain that God was pleased and the angels in heaven must have shouted with joy.

The world is full of people who wear nice clothes, live in beautiful homes, eat tasty food, and are starving for love. Several months ago a couple sat in my study trying to untangle the twisted strings of their marriage. They had been married for more than a decade and had three lovely children. I have always believed that two people who love each other and honestly seek God's guidance can find the answer to any problem in marriage. I always ask those who are trying to stop the leaks in the ship of matrimony if they love each other. I turned to the woman and asked, "Do you love your husband?" She replied without hesitation, "Yes, I love him." Then I turned to her husband and asked the same question. He looked down toward the floor, and then quickly glanced over toward his wife, and said, "I love her."

A few weeks later, the woman called me. "I want to thank you," she began, "for helping us through our little storm. You know," she continued, "that was the first time in over five years that I heard Bill say he loves me." I do not think, really, that it is necessary to go around verbally expressing our love for each other. On the other hand, we smother and stifle a lot of joy and happiness by suppressing our genuine feelings of affection toward those we love.

Suppose you knew for certain that you would live only one more day. What would you do with the last few fleeting hours of your life? How would you spend your last day? No doubt, some would spend it in prayer. Others would spend the precious hours with family and loved ones. Still others might take a trip. Probably a few would want to spend their last day doing the things they have always done. I have an idea that a host of people might like to spend the day saying to their loved ones and friends, "I love you."

While William L. Stidger was a student pastor in a little Cape Cod town, he lived with an old New England sea captain and his wife. One Saturday morning the woman died and Stidger did everything he could do to comfort the brokenhearted old man. All the time Stidger had lived with the couple he had never heard them express a kind or appreciative word to each other. Yet, Stidger said, he felt they genuinely loved and deeply respected each other. While William Stidger and the sea captain sat and talked, Stidger reminded him of his wife's willingness to help anybody who was ill or in distress. He spoke of her faithfulness and loyalty to God's Kingdom. She had been loyal with her time and talents and had given generously of her possessions to the church. The old sea captain sat and nodded in agreement to everything Stidger said.

After about two hours of talk, the old man looked the young minister in the eye and said, "I loved my wife—so much so that there were certain times when I came near telling her about it." I feel sure that his deceased wife knew that her husband loved her, but it would have brought gladness and happiness to her life if she could have heard him say, "I love you."

Love is not a barren virtue. Jesus said, "A good tree cannot bring forth evil fruit, neither can a corrupt tree bring forth good fruit. . . . Wherefore by their fruits ye shall know them" (MATTHEW 7:18-20). Genuine love is from God and it bears good fruit. Paul wrote, "Love knows no limit to its endurance, no end to its trust, no fading of its hope: it can outlast anything. It is, in fact, the one thing that still stands when all else has fallen" (I CORINTHIANS 13:7, PHILLIPS). I want to suggest five fruits which are evident in the lives of those who possess the greatest of all virtues, love.

(1) Love never fails; it can outlast anything. Paul wrote, "Charity never faileth . . ." (I CORINTHIANS 13:8). I have often wondered what Paul meant by that little phrase. It could be interpreted in at least two different ways. First, love never loses a battle; it always succeeds. We must admit that there are times when love appears to be defeated. Sometimes our own personal relationships become so confused and twisted that love seems to stand somewhere behind envy, jealousy and malice. Even in such times, who are we to suggest that love is beaten? It may be retreating, bending under the strain, but it is not really defeated. Second, Paul's phrase, "Charity never faileth," could be interpreted to mean that love never ends. Love never deserts us or falls down on the job. Genuine love, whether it be God's love for us or our love for one another, follows us no

117

matter where we go. Jesus said, ". . . and, lo, I am with you alway, even unto the end of the world" (MATTHEW 28:20).

A very sad story recorded in the New Testament makes it clear that Jesus never stops loving us. Once a very high-type citizen, a moral man, came to inquire of Jesus the requirements for eternal salvation. Jesus looked into the man's heart and in effect said, "You know what is required. You know the commandments as well as I do." The man responded by saying, "Master, all these have I observed from my youth" (MARK 10:20). Jesus advised him to sell his goods and give to the poor, but the poor fellow could not part with his earthly possessions. He did not wish to trade them even for eternal life. Jesus loved this man in spite of his unwillingness to part with his possessions: "Then Jesus beholding him loved him . . ." (MARK 10:21). The young man turned and walked slowly away. Make no mistake about it, the love of the Master followed him.

(2) Love never complains. Jesus lived a life of pure love. His deeds were never dingy with the desire for revenge. He loved everybody and His one desire was to have His Father's Kingdom of love reign in all human hearts. There is no record of Jesus' ever complaining.

I know a lady who waited on her sick husband for seven long years. During that time she was rarely out of the house. She spent many long, sleepless nights sitting by the side of his bed. She grew frail and thin, but, denying herself the proper rest, she waited with patience, understanding, and a love that was pure and strong. At the end of the seventh year, death claimed the man. Standing near the flower-decked casket with a saddened heart, hollow cheeks and trembling lips, his wife said, "Thank you, God, for giving me the strength to care for him until the end." That is love in its highest form.

(3) Not only is love uncomplaining, but love also endures. Paul said, "Love knows no limit to its endurance . . ." (1 CORINTHIANS 13:7, PHILLIPS). The King James Version says that love "Beareth all things." Genuine love has an eternal durability

that enables it to stand in the face of overwhelming opposition.

Look at the cross. Here we see love battered and bleeding, but not defeated. We see love bruised and mistreated, but not dead. Love was never more alive in the life of our Lord than when He died on the cross. On the cross, love was crucified and then buried in a tomb, but love can never be destroyed. It comes back to love again.

During my early ministry I saw God's love in a woman who was crushed, bruised and mercilessly beaten, only to rise above the hurt to love again. Almost every payday her husband came home without food or money. He was disgracefully drunk, and he usually clutched in his hand a half-filled liquor bottle. Often he beat his wife savagely, leaving her body bruised and her heart broken. The neighbors wondered why she did not leave him. Only those who knew her Christian fortitude and genuine love knew why she stayed and remained a good wife. When we are committed to God, and life is ordered by love, then, and only then, is one able to turn the other cheek.

(4) Love serves. "Love never asks how much must I do," wrote Frederick Agar, "but how much can I do." Christian love, in its concern for others, has sent men and women into the darkest jungles of the world. An army of Christian soldiers have given their lives to the cause of Christ. They have left the comfort of homes and stretched the ties of love to teach others about Christ. Many have marched to an early death with an unflagging faith in the love of God which compels Christian service.

Five young missionaries lost their lives a few years ago in the deep jungles of Ecuador. They flew their plane over a tribe of Auca Indians, dropping gifts and trying to express their friendly spirit and loving intentions. Soon after they landed, the savage Indians killed the dedicated men and their mutilated bodies were later found in a river. Some of the widows of the five missionaries chose to stay in Ecuador to help teach the children and soothe the fevered brows of the native Indians, teaching them at the same time about the love of God. Why did they decide to stay? The love of God had given them an irresistible desire to serve others.

When Sadhu Sundar Singh was converted to Christianity his parents used every strategy to get him to recant. Finally, they forced him to leave their house. This is how he described his first night out in the wilderness with nothing except the clothes on his back and a New Testament: "I spent the first night under a tree, shivering and hungry, but I remember the wonderful joy and peace in my heart; the presence of my Saviour. I held my New Testament in my hand and it was my first night in heaven."

Once when this great man was traveling with a guide in the Himalayas, they were caught in a heavy blizzard. They stumbled over a man who was almost dead and half covered with snow. The guide encouraged Singh to leave the man; to try to rescue him would imperil their own safety. The guide felt they must head for shelter with all haste.

While the guide hurried ahead, Singh stayed behind in an effort to rescue the dying man. He lifted him to his shoulders and battled the storm with his extra burden. Just before darkness, Singh saw the mouth of a cave ahead, a place for shelter and rest. Suddenly, Singh stumbled over the frozen body of the guide. Singh's body had been kept warm by his extra burden, and thereby his life was saved. It was his unfailing love for others that would not let him pass a dying man without making every effort to save him.

After the resurrection, Jesus asked Peter three times, ". . . lovest thou me?" (JOHN 21:15-17). Each time Peter responded in the affirmative. Jesus replied, "Feed my lambs. . . . Feed my sheep" (JOHN 21:15-16). I like to think that Jesus was saying to Peter, "If you really love Me, Peter, act as if you do." One positive proof of our devotion is seen in our Christian service. If we really have the love of God in our hearts, it will be reflected in our service to others. Some people love God with their lips, and others love God with their kind deeds of service.

(5) Christian love forgives. God's love in the human heart will span any chasm; it is deeper than adversity. It never gives way under the hurts others may inflict upon us. Love is never more beautiful than when it forgives. The person who holds in his heart an unforgiven hurt is not a genuine Christian. Jesus taught us to forgive, and if we would be like Him we must forgive those who disappoint and hurt us.

I once talked with a young girl who had committed a terrible wrong. She was afraid to tell her father. "If he finds it out," she confided in me, "he will probably beat me and never let me come back into his house." I told her I found it hard to believe that any father would treat his daughter in such a way. Later, I talked with the girl's father and he was deeply hurt and very determined. "She won't ever set her foot back in my house!" he said. "A daughter of mine who could do a thing like that can't ever live in my house," he continued.

"I know you are deeply disappointed," I said. "Your daughter has done wrong and she knows it. She has asked God to forgive her foolish and sinful act, and now she wants you to forgive her. Unless you are willing to forgive her," I continued, "God will not forgive your sins."

The man's wife, whose heart was crushed, pleaded with her husband. "We must stand by her. She needs our love." He thought about his own sins, and with tears in his eyes he said, "Tell her she can come back. I love her and I will forgive her." That is the kind of love we see expressed by the father of the prodigal son. That is the love we see expressed by Jesus. That is the kind of love you and I must express.

Christian love will open doors that logic and suspicion can never open. I have seen love stand battered but unbowed, bruised but unbeaten. Unless our love outlasts anything, unless it is uncomplaining, unless our love serves unselfishly, endures gladly and forgives completely, it is not like God's love. Unless our love is like God's love, we need to go back and stand at the foot of the cross and catch a fresh glimpse of His love; then go back to our homes, our places of work and our classrooms, and love our fellow man.

12

You Are Invited

ONE OF MY favorite verses in the Bible has been called "the great invitation": "Come unto me, all ye that labour and are heavy laden, and I will give you rest" (MATTHEW 11:28). Of course, Jesus was addressing those who labor to do the works of the law. Yet, the implications for present-day humanity run deeper. The yoke of sin and the burdens of sorrow, combined with the modern pace of living, cause teeming millions to become weary. There must be, on the road of life, some resting places. We need to renew our strength and refresh our energies.

Once, my secretary, who at the time was new on our staff, and who was trying to keep my work-load down, asked if I wanted to talk to everyone who called and asked to speak to me. I remembered our Lord, and how busy He was; yet He always had time to talk to the sick, the lame, the blind, and those in trouble. I thought about that great invitation, "Come unto me." My answer was simple, "When I am here, I will talk to anyone who calls." God called me into the ministry, and I don't want anyone to say that he called and I refused to talk with him. The door of my study is always open and God has never failed to give me the strength to do His work.

I like to go back to visit my mother and father. For several years my family and I lived so far away from Georgia that a visit more than once a year was impossible. Now we are less than a hundred miles from my parental home, and we often drive there late in the afternoon for dinner and a short visit. We do not need an invitation; most of the time we simply surprise my parents. Where love is genuine, one doesn't need an invitation. My parents always say, "Come every time you get an opportunity, even if it's just for a minute."

I do not like to be away from home any more than it is absolutely necessary. When my secretary is making plane reservations for me to fulfill an engagement, I always instruct her to arrange for me to be back home during the night, if possible. I have come into the Atlanta airport at every hour of the night and morning.

Recently I was in Jackson, Mississippi, waiting to board a plane. It was two-thirty in the morning. The man standing next to me remarked, "You are a minister from Atlanta, aren't you?" I replied, "Yes."

"What are you doing out here in the middle of the night?"

"I came out here to preach, and now I'm on my way home," I responded.

"I'm on an emergency trip," he volunteered, "or else I would be in bed, fast asleep."

I do not need an invitation to go home, and home is the place where love is real. This is true with the Master. You and I do not need to wait for a special invitation. Calvary is our special invitation. The Master follows us down the corridors of life saying, "Come unto me."

We spend a great deal of money having invitations engraved for weddings and other special occasions. Some people are excluded. This is not the case in the invitation Jesus gave. "Come unto me, all," said Jesus. You see, Jesus did not invite a special group. He invited humanity.

"Come unto me, all ye that labour and are heavy laden, and I will give you rest." What did Jesus mean by rest? He did not mean idleness; neither did He mean that we could relax and have a life of pure leisure. This is not a way around the demands of Christ; rather, it is a way through them. We are not to be freed from the cares of life, but we are to find rest as we bear the burdens of each day. Every person who honestly turns to Christ with his weary and burdened life will find rest. The storms may continue to lash the beaches of life; the winds of sorrow may blow against our sensitive hearts, and the burdens may press heavily upon our shoulders, but in it and through it all we can find in God a peace, confidence and strength that we never dreamed possible. All this is ours when we accept the invitation. Then, and only then, will we come to feel "the peace of God, which passeth all understanding . . ." (PHILIPPIANS 4:7).

I stood in the room of a very sick woman recently as she waited for the appointed time of surgery. Standing on one side of her bed was her husband; on the other side stood her brother. At the foot of the bed her mother stood, wiping tears from her eyes. These people were not members of the church I was serving, but someone had asked me to go by to see the sick woman.

I tried to bring a word of cheer to the anxious loved ones, and I talked to them about the love of God, reminding them of Paul's words: "I can do all things through Christ which strengtheneth me" (PHILIPPIANS 4:13). I think Paul also meant that he could face all things and bear all the burdens of life with complete confidence, and waving the flag of victory, through the strength of Christ.

After I offered a prayer, the patient spoke: "We don't have much hope of my coming through this operation, but we are not afraid, because we know that life is eternal, and if God doesn't let me stay here, He will surely take me home." With death near, hope of recovery fading, and only the flickering lamps of faith burning on the shores of eternity, this lovely Christian woman knew peace, confidence and rest. There was a glow on her face that told me that her faith was secure and her heart serene. She had accepted the invitation to come into the presence of God. She believed the promise, and found inner strength and rest.

I once talked with a very successful businessman who had more money and more misery than anyone I have ever known. For many months he had searched for rest and peace in a bottle. I told him that the Master offers rest: "If you come to Him and repent of your sins and live for God, you will be able to face the pressing problems of life. You won't need to crawl

125

into a bottle in an effort to escape life. You can live without a crutch, if you take Christ."

We prayed together and he left with hope in his heart and purpose in his life. Several months passed before I heard from him again. Late one night he called on the telephone. I thought he might be depressed, but he surprised me and said, "I just wanted to call and tell you that I have been reading my Bible and praying each day that God would give me the rest that He promised. I have found that rest, and I have joined the church."

Jesus also said, ". . . learn of me . . ." (MATTHEW 11:29). That is a mighty important phrase. It holds the key to finding the "rest" Jesus talks about. Let me suggest three things we need to learn about Jesus.

(1) Jesus was concerned about others. Too frequently we become wrapped up in our desires and personal ambitions, and we forget others. Jesus healed the lame and restored sight to the blind. He wanted to feed the hungry and clothe the naked. He was always eager to help those who needed Him.

There are millions of people who live in poverty. They have few clothes, little to eat, and many sleep out under the stars. Even though twenty centuries have passed since Jesus walked the dusty streets of Jerusalem, uncounted millions do not know God or the concern of Jesus for a struggling humanity. We would be more like our Lord if we could be as concerned as our Lord.

Jesus expressed this concern on the cross. He had been beaten and spat upon; His executioners pressed a crown of thorns on His head, and drove nails through His hands and feet. He hung in the burning sun until His lips were parched. But Jesus expressed concern for His mother. He looked down tenderly from the cross and into the loving eyes of His mother, ". . . and the disciple standing by, whom he loved, he saith unto his mother, Woman, behold thy son! Then saith he to the disciple, Behold thy mother!" (JOHN 19:26-27). With His last ounce of energy, Jesus was thinking not of Himself but of others.

126

Jesus was concerned about the thief on the cross. In His agony, He listened to the thief, with his penitent heart and pleading voice: "Lord, remember me when thou comest into thy kingdom. And Jesus said unto him, Verily I say unto thee, To day shalt thou be with me in paradise" (LUKE 23:42-43).

Our Lord even prayed for those who took His life. This is a clear manifestation of how we can love our enemies and pray for those who mistreat us.

(2) We need to learn obedience from Him: His major purpose was to do the will of His Father. Life was not easy for our Lord; neither is it easy for us; but Jesus obeyed God.

When life tumbles in, some people become bitter and turn against God. The truth is, they are turning against the only help that will heal the bleeding wounds of life.

(3) Jesus knew how to forgive. I do not know of anything more difficult than to forgive those who have done us an injustice. I only know that we must, and with God's help we can forgive. Our Lord said, "For if ye forgive men their trespasses, your heavenly Father will also forgive you: But if ye forgive not men their trespasses, neither will your Father forgive your trespasses" (MATTHEW 6:14-15).

One night a couple drove forty miles in a pouring rain to see me. They were making one last effort to save their marriage. "I have mistreated my wife," the husband began. "I have slapped her and I have been unfaithful to her. I don't know what caused me to do it. I really love her and I have asked God to forgive me, and now I am asking my wife to forgive me." We talked for a long time and had prayer. The sorrowful wife said, "I trusted him completely, and never dreamed that he was the kind of man who would strike me." She sat in the chair with her face in her hands, sobbing as if her heart would break. Here I saw evil and wrong mercilessly beating goodness and purity. I also saw the love and forgiveness of God cleaning the ugly wounds and covering them with the healing power of forgiveness. That wife, a mother of a beautiful child, prayed, "O God, I

127

want to forgive. Help me to forgive, even as You forgive us. Amen." She had learned a trying lesson. God had forgiven her many times and now she had learned to forgive someone who had hurt her.

John Maynard tells us about his own experience of being forgiven, and how he found Christ: "When I was a boy at school, I was mixed with some meanness and full of mischief. I enjoyed placing a frog in the teacher's desk or turning a pigeon loose in the classroom. I was the cause of several teachers' resigning and made it hard for the School Board to keep a teacher in the little red schoolhouse.

"Then one day a miracle happened. A lovely Christian, with a broad smile and a sense of humor, came to take over the school. She won my heart from the beginning. When I suddenly began to wash my face, comb my hair, and shine my shoes, my Mother and Father looked surprised.

"When commencement-time came, my parents received an invitation to come to the exercises. After the exercises were over the teacher invited the parents to look over the work of their children. When my parents walked over to look at my copybook, I hung my head. Before the new teacher came I had written on it upside down and put a few pictures in it. Finally, I peeped to see if Mother and Father were looking at my copybook. They were thumbing through it with a big smile on their faces. When they moved away, I tipped over to take a look and found someone had clipped all the ugly pages away, leaving only my best work. Then I felt the soft touch of a hand on my shoulder and I looked up into the face of my teacher. 'John, do you know who taught me how to do that?' As I shook my head she answered, 'Jesus taught me.' Then she asked me if I didn't want Jesus to wipe out all the ugly things in my past and forgive me. That is when I gave my life to Christ and He forgave my sins."

Jesus gives the invitation and we cannot be happy until we respond. "Come unto me, all ye that labour and are heavy laden, and I will give you rest."